FAMILY MOVIE NIGHT MENUS

TCM TURNER CLASSIC MOVIES

FAMILY MOVIE NIGHT MENUS

RECIPES & FILMS
FOR UNFORGETTABLE TIMES TOGETHER

LEONARD MALTIN
& JESSIE MALTIN

RUNNING PRESS
PHILADELPHIA

Page ii: Willy Wonka and the unforgettable Oompa-Loompas

Running Press
Hachette Book Group
1290 Avenue of the Americas, New York, NY 10104
www.runningpress.com
@Running_Press

First Edition: April 2026

Published by Running Press, an imprint of Hachette Book Group, Inc.
The Running Press name and logo are trademarks of Hachette Book Group, Inc.

The Hachette Speakers Bureau provides a wide range of authors for speaking events. To find out more, go to www.hachettespeakersbureau.com or email HachetteSpeakers@hbgusa.com.

Running Press books may be purchased in bulk for business, educational, or promotional use. For more information, please contact your local bookseller or the Hachette Book Group Special Markets Department at Special.Markets@hbgusa.com.

The publisher is not responsible for websites (or their content) that are not owned by the publisher.

Photo credits: cover: Shutterstock/aljosa2015; page 7: GettyImages/ucpage; page 22: GettyImages/LauriPatterson; page 30: GettyImages/mtreasure; page 14: Shutterstock/Jacek Chabraszewski; page 39: GettyImages/bhofack2; page 45: GettyImages/boblin; page 51: Shutterstock/Nature1000; page 58: Shutterstock/Dream79; page 66, top: Getty Images/LauriPatterson; page 66, bottom: GettyImages/Nature, food, landscape, travel; page 74: GettyImages/haoliang; page 80: GettyImages/Gary Quay; page 88: GettyImages/sbossert; page 96: GettyImages/LauriPatterson; page 104: GettyImages/EyeEm Mobile GmbH; page 111: Shutterstock/Aimee Lee Studios; page 126: Shutterstock/Hope Phillips; page 132: Shutterstock/from my point of view; page 161: Shutterstock/Brent Hofacker; page 168: GettyImages/LauriPatterson; page 177: GettyImages/Fudio; page 183: GettyImages/Ary6; all other images courtesy Turner Classic Movies, Inc.

Print book cover and interior design by Amanda Richmond

Library of Congress Cataloging-in-Publication Data
Names: Maltin, Leonard author | Maltin, Jessie, 1986– author | Turner Classic Movies (Firm) contributor Title: TCM family movie night menus : recipes & films for unforgettable times together / Leonard Maltin & Jessie Maltin. Other titles: Turner Classic Movies family movie night menus
Description: First edition. | Philadelphia : Running Press, 2026. | Includes index.
Identifiers: LCCN 2025036506 (print) | LCCN 2025036507 (ebook) | ISBN 9798894142371 hardcover | ISBN 9798894142388 ebook
Subjects: LCSH: Cooking | Motion pictures—Plots, themes, etc. | LCGFT: Cookbooks
Classification: LCC TX714 .M33755 2026 (print) | LCC TX714 (ebook) | DDC 641.5—dc23/eng/20250903
LC record available at https://lccn.loc.gov/2025036506
LC ebook record available at https://lccn.loc.gov/2025036507

ISBNs: 979-8-89414-237-1 (hardcover), 979-8-89414-238-8 (ebook)

Printed in China

1010

10 9 8 7 6 5 4 3 2 1

TO OUR PARTNERS,
ALICE AND SCOTT. MOVIES ARE
SO MUCH BETTER WHEN WE
WATCH THEM WITH YOU.

AND FOR DAISY,
THE LIGHT OF OUR LIVES.
WE CAN'T WAIT TO SHARE
ALL OF THIS WITH YOU.

CONTENTS

INTRODUCTION: MOVIE NIGHT DONE RIGHT xi

The Kid (1921) 1

Coogan Cakes 7

Bride of Frankenstein (1935) 9

German Goulash for the Monster in All of Us 15

Captain January (1936) 17

The Captain's Fish Sandwich 23

The Wizard of Oz (1939) 25

"Somewhere Over the Rainbow" Pizza 31

National Velvet (1944) 33

National Velvet Carrot Cake Cupcakes 38

Meet Me in St. Louis (1944) 41

Hickory Nut Cake 45

A Tree Grows in Brooklyn (1945) 47

Brooklyn Corned Beef and Cabbage 51

Singin' in the Rain (1952) 53

"Good Morning" Breakfast for Dinner 59

Calamity Jane (1953) 61
Calam's Biscuits 67

Seven Brides for Seven Brothers (1954). 69
Milly's Stick-to-Your-Ribs Stew 75

To Kill a Mockingbird (1962) 77
Harper Lee's Crackling Cornbread. 81

Mary Poppins (1964). 83
Pineapple Upside-Down Cake. 89

The Sound of Music (1965). 91
One of Maria's Favorite Things 97

Willy Wonka and the Chocolate Factory (1971) 99
Splendiferously Indulgent Cupcakes 105

Sounder (1972) 107
Doggone-Good Gumbo 111

Star Wars (1977) 113
Lightsaber Skewers 119

E.T. the Extra-Terrestrial (1982). 121
Chocolate Peanut Butter Pie 127

A Christmas Story (1983) 129
Christmas Stir-Fry 133

The Princess Bride (1987) 135
Toad-in-the-Hole 141

Honey, I Shrunk the Kids (1989) 143
Cheeri–OH NO! Bars 149

The Addams Family (1991). 151
Black-as-My-Soul Pasta. 155

The Secret Garden (1993) 157
Tea Party in the Garden. 161

A Little Princess (1995) 163
Chicken Tikka Masala 169

Harry Potter and the Sorcerer's Stone (2001) 171
Potter's Pumpkin Pasties. 177

Enchanted (2007). 179
Tempting (and Harmless) "Poison" Candy Apples. 183

ACKNOWLEDGMENTS. 184

INDEX 185

The deliciously devilish performances of Anjelica Huston and Raul Julia make *The Addams Family* a memorable film.

Glinda (Billie Burke) may have been a good witch, but we bet she never held a saucepan in her life.

INTRODUCTION

MOVIE NIGHT DONE RIGHT

THE GOAL: find a way to pass on our love of classic movies to the next generation.

THE MEANS: staging a series of family movie nights (or days) with recipes intended to put the whole clan in a good frame of mind.

JESSIE: *The greatest gift my parents gave me at an early age is a love of the arts (and a sense of humor). With their encouragement, I also came to appreciate the many people who collaborate to make a really good movie. In October 2021 I became a mother, and now I revel in sharing the things I love with my daughter. If I'm in the kitchen, she wants to cook with me. If I'm watching the Nicholas Brothers—as I often do—she can't help but try to dance along. Our time together is precious, and the thought of being able to help guide other families in a shared love of movies brings me an immense amount of joy.*

When I (Leonard) was growing up, television was still new, and the seven stations that operated in New York City became a living museum of movies. Vintage films of all kinds were pressed into service to entertain kids and grown-ups alike. I watched—no, I *absorbed*—Laurel and Hardy, The Little Rascals, and The Three Stooges on a daily basis. The repetition seared them into my consciousness, not to mention my heart. (Imagine how I felt when my only child was born on Stan Laurel's birthday and I received a greeting from Stan's daughter Lois, who sent along a check her father had written to her nanny in June of 1930.)

It isn't possible to duplicate my experience, but Jessie and I consulted with the good folks at TCM to assemble a roster of classic films—and what we think of as modern classics like *Star Wars*—in the hope of spawning a new generation of movie lovers. Jessie and I have collaborated on many projects over the years, but this is the first book that bears our names as official coauthors. From this point on, we will use the "royal we" except in describing a person I (Leonard) met or an incident I experienced without my writing partner.

To do all this in a normal-sized book meant we had to narrow our sights. We decided not to attempt to cover the vast field of animation, along with the work of Walt Disney, whose family appeal is obvious. We also omitted the foundational comedies starring Buster Keaton, Harold Lloyd, *Our Gang (The Little Rascals)*, and The Marx Brothers. Those are enormous subjects worthy of entire books. (I have even written some of them!) But we had to include one emblematic silent comedy and easily chose *The Kid* (1921) with Charlie Chaplin and the adorable Jackie Coogan, a family-friendly film if there ever was one.

I married a woman who shares my love of movies. Alice and I were blessed with the arrival of our daughter Jessie in June of 1986. She in turn gave us a glorious granddaughter in October of 2021. I can't wait to start showing movies to little Daisy . . . all in good time.

I clearly remember some specific choices Alice and I made as Jessie was growing up. She was three and a half years old when my wife's all-time favorite movie, *Seven Brides for Seven Brothers* (1954), was released on LaserDisc. (The medium never caught on and was soon supplanted by DVDs and Blu-ray Discs, but at that time it was a leap ahead of videocassettes because you could hop to any moment in the film in a nanosecond.) That day, we showed Jessie the barn-raising segment of *Seven Brides*, and she stood in front of our large-screen television, transfixed. "Again," she commanded, and I obliged. "Again," she repeated, and I cued up the production number once more.

After watching that one sequence countless times she eventually showed some curiosity about who the characters were and how they arrived at this barn-raising ceremony. She fell in love with the 1954 musical, just like my wife, whose telephone ring is Howard Keel singing a song from the picture.

While pondering what to show Jessie next, a copy of *Calamity Jane* (1953) crossed my desk. "She'll love watching a tomboy character," I thought to myself, and besides, she'll recognize Doris Day's leading man from *Seven Brides*, Howard Keel. After that I brought home yet another Doris Day musical, *The Pajama Game* (1957) and it became another favorite. This ploy worked for quite a while. (We all love musicals in this household.)

Because we hadn't screened any clunkers, Jessie was pretty open-minded about the musicals we chose to share. She fell in love with Ginger Rogers and Fred Astaire and especially liked Donald O'Connor in *Singin' in the Rain* (1952). Who *doesn't*?

I came to realize that once you introduce your children to "the good stuff," they will recognize it on their own and reject what some of their peer group may be embracing. Our daughter was ten or so when MTV came along, and we didn't stop her from watching it in her room. I never wanted her to live in the past. She came to me after a while and said she thought a lot of the videos were sexist. I congratulated her for figuring that out on her own.

We also had the good fortune of bringing her to a series of silent-film showings with live musical accompaniment. That's how she was introduced to Chaplin, Keaton, and Lloyd. Watching a silent comedy at home without an audience is less than ideal, but it's the most practical solution for most families. If there's any way to invite friends to join you for the screening, it will pay big dividends.

Jessie: *Don't overexplain. If it's a silent movie, just tell them that there won't be any dialogue. Just let them enjoy it. When they have questions, answer them. Kids are a lot more open than most adults, and they'll watch stuff. While watching The Marx Brothers in* Horse Feathers *(1932) or* A Night at the Opera *(1935), it doesn't matter if young ones don't "get" Groucho's jokes. It's the rhythm and timing of his wisecracks that makes them so funny... and meanwhile, young viewers can revel in the silliness of the ever-silent Harpo.*

This is especially true when they are little. Get 'em young and get them hooked on the good stuff.

Jessie remains an individual with her own inimitable style and mindset. She can quote every word of *Con Air* (1997) and would die for Nicolas Cage but will always cite *Seven Brides for Seven Brothers* as her all-time favorite movie. She regards the movies she grew up with as "comfort food."

We're not pretending that the twenty-five films in this book are the best of all time. We offer them as a sampling of good movies you can enjoy as a family and talk about afterwards. We encourage you to use them as starting points to chart your own journey through the world of cinema. And why go hungry while you're watching? We hope our recipes will add to the experience of family movie night.

KIDS, DON'T TRY THIS AT HOME–WITHOUT A GROWN-UP

These recipes often involve very hot ovens, careful mixing of ingredients in bowls, and other tasks that young children should not undertake without adult supervision. When it comes to eating the finished product, everyone can join in . . . but don't try anything straight out of the oven. Let it cool down first.

Hollywood's unsung hero: Toto from *The Wizard of Oz*

An iconic image of Charlie Chaplin and Jackie Coogan; the cop is Chaplin regular Tom Wilson.

THE KID

(1921)

68 MINUTES

Written and directed by Charles Chaplin
Cast: Charles Chaplin, Jack Coogan, Edna Purviance, Carl Miller, Albert Austin, Henry Bergman, Jack Coogan Sr., Charles Reisner, Tom Wilson, Lita Grey

Charlie Chaplin's Little Tramp is a timeless and universal figure. Every member of your family should get to know him because he built the foundation of what we know as comedy in the movies.

If your family doesn't already know Chaplin, *The Kid* is a great place to start because it features the incredibly charming Jackie Coogan (officially billed on screen as Jack). The five-year-old costar is beautifully showcased in this short feature film, running just about an hour and written especially with him in mind. With his oversized cap and ragamuffin outfit, he is definitely a "have-not," which immediately inspires sympathy for him. He and Charlie live in what might be called a garret and have a pretty clever working partnership. Jackie throws rocks at windowpanes, and Charlie happens along just when a prospective customer is in need of a glazier. A neighborhood bully notifies the authorities of Jackie's existence without proper supervision, which sends a truant officer his way and leads to a heart-tugging scene in which the little boy cries out for the only daddy he's ever known.

The Kid promises "a laugh, perhaps a tear," which sets it apart from virtually every other comedy of the silent-film era. No one explored the idea of pathos as doggedly, or as successfully, as Chaplin. He made people fall in love with his dignified hobo and care about him so much that he could even break

A bond that no one can break

their hearts. The process reached its peak in his 1931 gem *City Lights*, but *The Kid* was his first feature to openly aim for this result. Indeed, it was his first starring feature film.

Who wouldn't be moved by the plight of Charlie and Jackie when the "bad guys" show up and take the boy? In a beautifully choreographed sequence, Charlie clambers over rooftops to catch up with the truck that's carrying Jackie.

This is preceded by a wonderful set piece showing a typical morning in the lives of this loving duo. Jackie is making and stacking pancakes on a hot plate, while Charlie is still in the process of waking up. It's a picture of blissful domesticity, which makes the arrival of the truant officer all the more upsetting.

Charlie's longtime leading lady, Edna Purviance, appears as the unwed mother who gives birth to Jackie and then abandons him in the back seat of an expensive automobile with a handwritten note: "Please love and care for this orphan child." The chauffeur who returns to the vehicle wants nothing to do with the baby and pawns him off on another sucker, until he winds up in the arms of Charlie.

There are few title cards in the film because the action speaks for itself in almost every scene. Even when Edna is released from the maternity hospital and the camera lingers on two cynical-looking employees, we can imagine what they say to each other; we don't need a road map.

When you witness an artist like Chaplin at his peak, you understand why he was loved around the globe. He began making films in 1914 for the rough-and-ready comedy producer Mack Sennett, and within months his likeness on a sidewalk standee was all it took to lure an audience into a theater. "He's Here Today," a sign would proclaim, and people responded enthusiastically. Chaplin became the most well-known human being on the planet at a time when there was no television or even radio, let alone an internet, to spread the word of his gifts. A shy, unassuming member of British impresario Fred Karno's knockabout comedy troupe, he was recommended to Sennett during an American tour, and the producer hired him without even seeing him perform. Back then, it would take about a week to piece together a comedy produced by Sennett and the Keystone Film Company, and Charlie was a quick learner. Before long he was directing his own short subjects and working closely with such collaborators as Mabel Normand and Roscoe "Fatty" Arbuckle.

Sennett's comedies aren't subtle; sometimes the gags are downright crude, but Chaplin brought his own ideas to the fore and quickly established his screen persona as the Little Tramp, whose

Charlie meets an angel in this daring dream sequence. He would eventually marry Lita Grey, the young actress in this scene.

Breakfast is no simple matter for the Little Tramp and the Kid.

ill-fitting clothes indicate the kind of gentleman he aspires to be. The setting for most of his films is an unidentified pocket of urban poverty, inspired by the places in London that he actually grew up around. Memories of those squalid neighborhoods never left his consciousness, and he revisited them in the sets he built on his studio lot.

After one year he was lured away by the Essanay Film Manufacturing Company, headquartered in Chicago, for a then-astonishing $1,250 a week, and just twelve months later he signed with Mutual Film Corporation for $675,000 per year.

If you're just getting to know Chaplin, the Sennett shorts are mostly primitive and only watchable for purposes of study and context. The Essanay shorts are much better. But the "golden dozen" two-reelers he made for Mutual from 1916 to 1917 are among his all-time finest work. You would be hard-pressed to find twenty-minute shorts as funny and inventive as *Easy Street*, *The Immigrant*, *The Cure*, *Behind the Screen*, *The Pawnshop*, *The Adventurer*, *The Rink*, or *One A.M.*

If curiosity sets in and you want to learn more about this pantomime genius of early Hollywood, it is imperative that you see Kevin Brownlow and David Gill's three-part television documentary *Unknown Chaplin* (1983). Using hundreds of outtakes that miraculously survived the years, we see how Chaplin developed an idea, rehearsed it on film (with his trusty cinematographer Rollie Totheroh hand-cranking the camera), and refined it through seemingly endless repetition. He was seeking nothing less than perfection, and as often as not attained it.

An original lobby card for *The Kid*, now more than one hundred years old

Charlie built his own studio in Hollywood on La Brea Boulevard, and it still stands. In fact, it was owned for many years by Jim Henson's company, which put a drawing of Kermit the Frog as Chaplin on its signage. Owning his own studio meant that if Charlie wasn't inspired to create comedy on a given morning, he didn't, and he would send everyone on staff home for the day. The studio was his home base right through the early 1950s, when he completed filming *Limelight* (1952) there. He wisely retired the Little Tramp when sound came to Hollywood. After all, because he never spoke, he was just as popular in Nigeria as he was in Niagara Falls. If he spoke, he would risk his universality. Chaplin dodged the issue altogether by making two final silent films in the midst of a talkie hurricane: *City Lights* and *Modern Times*. He composed music scores for both and even sang a gibberish song in the latter film. And because it was Charlie Chaplin, people turned out to see him.

The Kid was in production for the better part of a year. In fact, First National Pictures used this fact to promote the picture. The one-sheet poster declared, "This is the great film he has been working on for a whole year."

Meanwhile, his first marriage, to Mildred Harris, was dissolving. You can see who took her place in Charlie's affections in *The Kid*. During the climactic dream sequence—another innovative concept—she is the only girl who gets a close-up: Lita Grey.

As for Jackie Coogan, few actors ever had a launchpad as fruitful as *The Kid*.

Jackie was a sensation, and with his parents making film and merchandise deals left and right, he remained a star into the talkie era. Coogan was four years old when Chaplin discovered him dancing a shimmy onstage at the Los Angeles Orpheum Theatre. He turned five during the extended production time the writer-director-star spent on this endeavor. Jackie starred in silent-film versions of *Peck's Bad Boy* (1921) and *Oliver Twist* (1922) and played other famous juvenile characters. He was also the first child star to be licensed for a wide array of products ranging from peanut butter to stationery. As he outgrew his cuteness in the 1930s, Coogan's career cooled and could best be described as sporadic from that point on. Baby boomers will remember him as the chubby, bald-headed Fester in the 1960s TV series *The Addams Family*.

In 1975, he attended a screening of *The Kid* at that year's Cinecon convention. It was screened in the Blossom Ballroom of the Hollywood Roosevelt Hotel, literally walking distance from the Chaplin studio. His young grandson Keith (who later pursued a film career) was in attendance. When it came time for a Q and A, I raised my hand and said, "Here we are, more than fifty years since the film was made, so close to where you shot it. Your family is here with you. What goes through your mind as you watch it?" He replied, "I think about the money." It was not the answer I expected, and I think it brought everybody down—glad we had a chance to cheer for him in person but saddened by the realization that his parents' recklessness affected him for the rest of his life. His name is still invoked because of California's Coogan Law, which attempted to protect the earnings of minors from greedy parents and guardians.

Fortunately, you and your family can enjoy watching two special performers working beautifully together without the shadow of later problems clouding it. *The Kid* stands up today.

Coogan Cakes

The image of Jackie Coogan making pancakes for Charlie Chaplin is one that always makes us smile. The sweetness, the innocence (and the stealing of bites as you go). Let's make some old-fashioned pancakes.

MAKES 4 SERVINGS

2 cups all-purpose flour

3½ teaspoons baking powder

1 teaspoon kosher salt

1 tablespoon granulated sugar

Sprinkle of cinnamon

1¼ cups whole milk

1 large egg

3 tablespoons butter, melted

1 tablespoon vanilla extract

Small amount of vegetable oil to coat skillet

In a large bowl, combine the dry ingredients: flour, baking powder, salt, sugar, and cinnamon. In a separate medium bowl, combine the wet ingredients: milk, egg, butter, and vanilla extract. Gently whisk the wet ingredients into the dry until just combined. Do not over-stir.

Heat the vegetable oil in a large skillet over medium heat. Pour the batter into the skillet, about ¼ cup per pancake. The most important thing we've learned about pancakes—a phrase we didn't think we'd use in our lifetimes—is that you've got to wait for bubbles. When you see bubbles forming, that's the perfect time to flip that puppy over.

Brown on both sides and serve hot.

Heggie plays the blind hermit who becomes the Creature's only friend.

BRIDE OF FRANKENSTEIN

(1935)

75 MINUTES

Directed by James Whale | **Produced by** Carl Laemmle Jr.
Screenplay by William Hurlbut | **Cinematography by** John J. Mescall
Cast: Boris Karloff, Colin Clive, Valerie Hobson, Elsa Lanchester, Ernest Thesiger, E. E. Clive, O. P. Heggie, Dwight Frye

There are few stories as durable as Mary Shelley's *Frankenstein.* The tale of a mad scientist who wants to bring a dead body to life—but inadvertently inserts a damaged brain in its skull—has inspired storytellers for two hundred years. His name has become part of our language, even though we use the name to refer to the monster and not the man who created him.

Four years after *Frankenstein* (1931) broke new ground and established the horror film as a viable genre, Universal decided to make a sequel—as rare then as it is commonplace today. What's more, the studio hired the same director, James Whale, to pilot the follow-up and the same actors to play the mad scientist (Colin Clive) and the monster (Boris Karloff). But in the four years between these assignments, Boris Karloff had become a star; he even played the title role in the studio's 1932 hit *The Mummy.* Adding to his mystique, he is billed merely as Karloff in the opening titles.

Normally, we wouldn't be highlighting the second film in a series, but there are many reasons for your family to watch *Bride of Frankenstein* before sampling the original. An early talkie, *Frankenstein* has an arid soundtrack and no music score. The lavish sequel moves at a brisk pace and contains unforgettable vignettes, not to mention Elsa Lanchester as both Mary Wollstonecraft Shelley, in a prologue, and the mate Dr. Frankenstein fashions for his misbegotten monster. (Interestingly, in the opening titles the actress playing his mate is left as a question mark.)

James Whale liked big sets, and his gifted art director Charles D. Hall gave him just what he wanted, even though the film doesn't spend much time in them. In contrast, the forest, which is shown repeatedly in silhouette, seems not quite real.

The highly eccentric Ernest Thesiger, who was introduced to American audiences in James Whale's *The Old Dark House* (1932), appears as Dr. Pretorius, who boasts that he was "booted out" of medical

school, and proudly shows off his laboratory experiments: human beings shrunk to miniature size. He wants to collaborate with Dr. Frankenstein, but the good doctor wants nothing to do with further experiments. The development of visual effects since 1935 hasn't diminished the fascination with seeing humans reduced to the size of dolls and put on display under glass.

As for the unsuspecting bride, she is played to perfection by character actress Elsa Lanchester, whose image—with a streak of white accenting her outsized hairdo—is known to countless people who may not realize its origin. The camera surveys the contours of her face and the reactions of the others in the lab in a rapidly edited sequence that is a tour de force. If it is still striking today, imagine how moviegoers must have responded back in 1935.

Elsa Lanchester achieved immortality as **the Bride**, fashioned by makeup wizard Jack Pierce and director James Whale.

One of the most memorable and moving scenes in the first film shows the creature drowning a little girl because he thinks she will float, like the flower petals she's been casting into a lake. This depiction of the monster as an innocent is further explored in *Bride*, where he speaks for the first time. The spur for this is an unforgettable vignette featuring character actor O. P. Heggie as a blind hermit who lives in the forest. He speaks to the monster without fear because he can't see him. As they begin to form a friendship the reason becomes clear: they are *both* innocents. Karloff's childlike pantomime reaches its zenith in this famous scene, where his host's violin-playing elicits tears from the so-called monster.

Although it's surprisingly short (just an hour and fifteen minutes), there's a lot to digest and a great deal to discuss after a screening. Was it a good idea to give

the monster the ability to speak? (He is mute in the original film, though he talks in the Shelley novel and even demands a mate.) How did the craftspeople fashion Dr. Frankenstein's laboratory without the benefit of computer-generated imagery (CGI)? Did you realize that the Bride is played by the same woman who appears in the opening scene as author Mary Wollstonecraft Shelley?

Let's not overlook the colorful character actors who populate the film, including excitable Una O'Connor as Minnie, the skittish housekeeper; O. P. Heggie as the blind hermit; E. E. Clive as the burgomaster; and the always-eerie Dwight Frye as Karl, Dr. Frankenstein's crazed assistant (called Fritz in the earlier film).

Finally, once you and your family have digested *Bride of Frankenstein*, you will have decide when you want to share Mel Brooks's brilliant parody, *Young Frankenstein* (1974) with them. Some of the more suggestive humor will probably sail over their heads, and there is nothing objectionable. If anything, *Young Frankenstein* will help sharpen their sense of humor and give them a taste of screen comedy at its finest and funniest. They may also recognize Gene Wilder (who shares writing credit with Brooks) as the star of *Willy Wonka and the Chocolate Factory*, if you're smart enough to choose the 1971 version of Roald Dahl's famous story to show them.

Elsa Lanchester bookends this ingenious film, appearing at the very beginning (as Mary Shelley) and at the end (as the Bride).

German Goulash for the Monster in All of Us

Nothing warms up the soul quite like Rindergulasch (say that five times fast). No monster can resist this delicious delicacy.

MAKES 4 SERVINGS

3 pounds beef chuck, cubed

2 teaspoons kosher salt, divided

¾ teaspoon freshly ground black pepper, divided

¼ cup vegetable oil, divided

2 yellow onions, chopped

2 cloves garlic, minced

1½ tablespoons sweet paprika

1 tablespoon all-purpose flour

1⅓ cups red wine

2 cups beef broth, plus more as needed

¼ cup tomato paste

½ teaspoon dried rosemary

1 tablespoon red wine vinegar

1 large carrot, chopped

1 large red bell pepper, chopped

1 large yellow bell pepper, chopped

3 tablespoons fresh parsley, minced

Toss the beef chuck with 1 teaspoon of salt and ¼ teaspoon of black pepper. Let sit for 15 minutes.

In a large pot, heat 2 tablespoons of the vegetable oil over medium-high heat. When the oil shimmers, add ⅓ of the beef cubes and brown on all sides. Remove to a plate and repeat with remaining beef. Moderate heat so brown bits on the bottom of the pan do not burn, and add more oil as necessary. Remove all but 2 tablespoons oil from the pot and discard.

Reduce heat to medium-low and add onion to the pot. Sauté until the onion begins to soften, about 4 to 5 minutes. Add garlic and sauté, stirring frequently.

Sprinkle paprika and flour over the onions and garlic and sauté over medium heat, stirring constantly, for 1 minute.

Pour in wine and bring to a boil. Stir and remove all brown bits on the bottom of the pan. When the liquid boils, reduce heat and add the beef broth, tomato paste, rosemary, red wine vinegar, 1 teaspoon salt, and ½ teaspoon black pepper.

Return the browned beef along with any accumulated juices to the pot. Bring to a boil, then reduce heat and simmer, uncovered, about 2 to 2½ hours or until beef is fork-tender.

Add carrot and peppers and simmer until vegetables are tender. If the liquid becomes too thick, add more beef broth or water to thin. (The liquid should be like gravy.) Adjust seasoning as needed, sprinkle with parsley, then ladle into individual bowls and serve.

Shirley and Buddy Ebsen dance to the strains of “At the Codfish Ball.”

CAPTAIN JANUARY

(1936)

77 MINUTES

Directed by David Butler | **Produced by** B. G. DeSylva
Screenplay by Sam Hellman, Gladys Lehman, Harry Tugend;
based on a story by Laura E. Richards | **Cinematography by** John Seitz
Musical direction by Cyril J. Mockridge | **Songs by** Lew Pollack and Sidney D. Mitchell | **Production design by** William Darling | **Cast:** Shirley Temple, Guy Kibbee, Slim Summerville, Buddy Ebsen, Sara Haden, Jane Darwell, June Lang, Jerry Tucker, Nella Walker, George Irving, Si Jenks, Billy Benedict

One of the biggest stars of the 1930s was actually quite small: Shirley Temple. Ninety years after her heyday, she remains a wonder to behold. Shirley was one of a kind: at three years old she was able to learn lines and complicated choreography, "sell" the songs she was given to sing, and hold her own opposite some of the most imposing actors in Hollywood. Living with a toddler in our house, we marvel all the more at Shirley's immense and precocious talent. Her films may be old, but she is forever young—and absolutely captivating. She is much more than a nonalcoholic beverage.

She was featured in a handful of short subjects and feature films before her breakthrough came in 1934's *Baby, Take a Bow*, in which she performed her soon-to-be signature song, "On the Good Ship Lollipop." She endeared herself to audiences of all ages and became world-famous, a celebrity that every visitor to Los Angeles wanted to meet. By 1936, when *Captain January* was made, she was at the peak of her career. She was just eight years old.

Well-known character actor Guy Kibbee plays the title role, an "old salt" known as Cap, who operates a lighthouse at Cape Tempest, Maine, and looks after his curly-headed charge named Star (Temple). Her parents drowned in a shipwreck, and she has lived with Cap ever since. An obnoxious and persistent woman (Sara Haden) wants to save her from the supposedly negative influence of Cap and his seagoing friends, but in fact Star has learned to read and write quite well. When the situation seems hopeless, Cap's pal Nazro (Slim Summerville) writes to a man in Boston whose name he found in a scrapbook he saved from the sinking ship. At the same time, new electronic equipment is being installed in the lighthouse that will put Cap out of work. How will it all end?

The writers who crafted this star vehicle for Shirley knew what the audience expected: a warm relationship with a grown-up (preferably a parent but sometimes a father figure) and a crisis or problem that had to be solved. Watching Shirley being hauled away from her beloved Cap, crying out for him, is tough going for anyone, regardless of age. The scene also demands complete sincerity from her costar, and Guy Kibbee was fully up to the task.

There have been child stars before and since, but Shirley was seen as a beacon of happiness and light in the depths of the Great Depression of the 1930s. Her studio often paired her with older character actors like Kibbee and long-faced Slim Summerville, who didn't mind competing with her effortless scene-stealing ways—and had more than a few tricks up their sleeves. She memorized not only her lines but also everybody's in the script, which caused occasional embarrassment to the actor who forgot their dialogue. She took direction well, especially from veterans like David Butler, who steered her to success in four of her best movies: *Bright Eyes* (1934), *The Little Colonel* (1935), *The Littlest Rebel* (1935), and *Captain January*. (The musical numbers here were staged by Jack Donohue.)

She danced most memorably with Bill "Bojangles" Robinson in *The Little Colonel* and *The Littlest Rebel*, and while those numbers (which involved going up and down a flight of steps) are still impressive, the films in which they appear are problematic for twenty-first-century viewers. They glorify the Old South in a way that makes *Gone with the Wind* seem tame by comparison. But if you and your family become Shirley Temple fans—which may well happen—you should watch those films with a lot of caveats. Discussing white America's attitudes toward Black people, segregation,

Shirley and Guy Kibbee, who plays the title role in *Captain January*

and the Jim Crow South can stimulate and educate young people on a broader scale and open doors to watching other twentieth-century films that might otherwise be taboo. Give it a try.

No one could approach Bill Robinson in terms of tap technique and showmanship, and it's heartwarming to learn that Shirley Temple and her family welcomed him into their home for Sunday dinners numerous times. Few Black entertainers were treated with that kind of friendship and respect by white families in Hollywood.

In *Captain January*, Shirley's dancing partner is lanky, loose-limbed Buddy Ebsen, and their delightful partnership is also worth celebrating as they perform "At the Codfish Ball." It's an extended song and dance that's so enjoyable you don't want it to end.

Ebsen was originally cast as the Tin Man in *The Wizard of Oz* (1939) but had to be replaced when he had a bad reaction to the silver makeup he was required to wear. He is best remembered as Davy Crockett's sidekick George Russell in the hugely successful Walt Disney TV shows and movies of the 1950s, and for his starring roles in two long-running television series, *The Beverly Hillbillies* in the 1960s and *Barnaby Jones* in the 1970s. Many followers of those TV shows had no inkling that he had made his reputation decades earlier as a dancer, often working with his sister Vilma.

Guy Kibbee was a very busy man throughout the 1930s, taking the leading role in the Warner Bros.' adaptation of the Nobel Prize–winning Sinclair Lewis novel *Babbitt* (1934) and playing mostly comedic bumblers in such films as *42nd Street* (1933), *Lady for a Day* (1933), *Captain Blood* (1935), *Mr. Smith Goes to Washington* (1939), and *Our Town* (1940). He also played Scattergood Baines, a character introduced in the *Saturday Evening Post* by author Clarence Buddington Kelland, in six B movies of the early 1940s.

Yet not even Hollywood's greatest producers and visual effects wizards could keep Shirley from growing older, and as she did, she lost some of the impish charm that made her so well-loved. She continued making movies into the early 1940s and even received her first screen kiss (in 1942's *Miss Annie Rooney*, from fellow adolescent Dickie Moore). But when she was twelve her mother enrolled her in the prestigious private Westlake School for Girls in Los Angeles, marking the first time she had ever been in a classroom with other girls. Looking back, she felt that this radical change just as she was approaching puberty was a lifesaver and kept her feet firmly on the ground.

If your family shows interest in what happened to the real-life Shirley Temple, we encourage you to read her fascinating autobiography, *Child Star*. In it we learn how she viewed her celebrity and some of the pitfalls that went along with it. She knew that she was doing a job and favored the actors, directors, and crew members who treated her as a colleague, not a moppet. Her child's-eye view of the world is compelling. She judged most men by their shoes.

She learned diplomacy at a tender age, making her later career in that field seem entirely appropriate. She also learned some hard lessons, as when she discovered that the fortune she had earned, not only from her salary but from the sale

Sara Haden (right) threatens to separate Shirley from her beloved guardian. Slim Summerville, Shirley, and Guy Kibbee listen but don't like what they're hearing.

of Shirley Temple dolls, had been squandered by her well-meaning father, who worked in a bank but had less-than-stellar luck in his choice of investments. When she came of age and was told that she had less than $20,000, she could have sued her father—which she refused to even consider—or she could take a deep breath and start all over again, not unlike the can-do optimists she played so often on-screen.

I (Leonard) had the great good fortune to meet and interview Shirley Temple in her home in Hillsboro, California, on two occasions, and she couldn't have been more gracious. She didn't live in the past but didn't mind talking about it. I also got to see her give one of her grandchildren a lesson in dancing the time step!

It is worth noting that *Captain January* was the second time this story was filmed. The first version, a decade earlier, featured one of the top child stars of the silent era, Baby Peggy. She, too, wound up writing an autobiography as well as other books about Hollywood in the early days. She even penned a first-rate biography of Jackie Coogan, the only tyke to outdo her in the public's affection during the 1920s. All of this was under her real name, Diana Serra Cary. She lived to be 101 years old and participated in tributes to her once-forgotten career as prints of her starring films were discovered and restored. She deserves to be rediscovered by families of today.

The Captain's Fish Sandwich

When you're longing for something salty and fresh, a fish sandwich is the way to go. You can even make a Shirley Temple to go with it.

MAKES 4 SANDWICHES

FOR THE TARTAR SAUCE:

1 small white onion, minced

1 garlic clove, minced

2 teaspoons chives, minced

1 medium scallion, minced

½ cup mayonnaise

1 tablespoon white wine vinegar

1 tablespoon olive oil

1 tablespoon capers

Juice from 2 lemons

Kosher salt and freshly ground black pepper

FOR THE FISH PATTIES:

13 ounces cod or haddock

3 large eggs, divided

1 cup panko crumbs, divided

½ teaspoon paprika

½ teaspoon garlic powder

½ teaspoon onion powder

1 teaspoon kosher salt

½ teaspoon freshly ground black pepper

¼ cup flour

Olive oil to coat skillet

FOR THE SANDWICHES:

4 brioche buns

1 large tomato, sliced

Alfalfa sprouts, for garnish

Combine all ingredients for the tartar sauce. Set aside.

Now for our fish patties. Cut your fish up and put it into a blender. Blend until it's close to a paste, then transfer to a bowl.

Add 1 egg and 3 tablespoons panko crumbs to the bowl and mix in with your hands. Add the paprika, garlic powder, onion powder, salt, and pepper. Mix in again. In a separate bowl, combine 2 eggs and the remaining panko crumbs.

Sprinkle the flour on a wooden board so your fish won't stick. Carefully start to form patties with your hands. Dip them in the egg/panko mixture, then place them on the wooden board.

Heat the olive oil in a large skillet or sauté pan over medium-high heat. Cook the patties for about 5 minutes on each side. Remove from heat and add a little lemon juice on top if you like.

Spread the buns with tartar sauce and add a slice of tomato and some alfalfa sprouts. Place your patty on top.

Dorothy Gale dreams of a happy place over the rainbow in the sepia-tinted opening sequence of *The Wizard of Oz*, directed (without credit) by King Vidor. It was not uncommon for MGM to bring on other talent when the primary director was busy.

THE WIZARD OF OZ

(1939)

101 MINUTES

Directed by Victor Fleming | **Produced by** Mervyn LeRoy
Screenplay by Noel Langley, Florence Ryerson, Edgar Allan Woolf
Cinematography by Hal Rosson | **Musical direction by** Herbert Stothart
Songs by Harold Arlen and E. Y. Harburg | **Cast:** Judy Garland, Ray Bolger, Jack Haley, Bert Lahr, Frank Morgan, Billie Burke, Margaret Hamilton, Charley Grapewin, Clara Blandick

In late 2024, a private collector paid $28 million for a prop from a classic movie made more than eighty years ago. The bounty was the ruby slippers from *The Wizard of Oz*, a rare example of a classic film that has never left the psyche or the hearts of its many fans. *Wicked* is just the latest variation on the original story, based on L. Frank Baum's 125-year-old book.

The story centers on a Kansas girl named Dorothy Gale who yearns for a more colorful life than the one she leads on her drab family farm. She wishes she were over the rainbow, in a magical place that forms in her imagination. Suddenly, a tornado erupts all around her and a piece of debris knocks her out cold. When she awakens, she finds herself in Oz, where her house has landed upon (and killed) the Wicked Witch of the East—making her a heroine to the resident Munchkins. They advise her to follow the yellow brick road to the Emerald City, where she will find the wizard, who can send her safely back home. Along the way she meets a rusted Tin Man who wants a heart, an overworked Scarecrow who wishes he had a brain, and a Cowardly Lion who yearns for the one thing he lacks: courage. They lock arms and head off together to see the wonderful wizard who can make their dreams come true. Naturally, complications arise.

Glinda the Good Witch (Billie Burke) tries to protect Dorothy (Judy Garland) from the Wicked Witch of the West (Margaret Hamilton).

This 1939 feature is about as perfect as any film can hope to be. It's certainly one of the most quoted movies of all time. "Pay no attention to that man behind the curtain." "Toto, I've a feeling we're not in Kansas anymore." "And your little dog, too." You're as likely to hear one of those dialogue snippets in a television episode as you are in everyday conversation. How many older films have retained that level of awareness in a generation that wasn't born when it first appeared?

One reason this lavish fantasy holds up so well is that it doesn't talk down to its audience; its screenplay is intelligent and witty. Another major aspect is the once-in-a-lifetime cast, led by sixteen-year-old Judy Garland. She was nothing like Dorothy in real life, so what you're seeing is a beautifully sincere performance. When she sings "Over the Rainbow," you believe every word of it. And when she starts traveling on that yellow brick road, you're right alongside her.

A few safety warnings for parents of young children: there are some scary scenes involving the Wicked Witch of the West and her army of flying monkeys, and a nightmarish sequence in which trees in the forest come to life. But like many such films, this one includes frightening moments to make its heartfelt story that much richer and deeper.

Next, a strong suggestion: *The Wizard of Oz* has been examined more closely than almost any other movie of its time.

Entire books have been written about its creation, but don't let your family read anything before they see it. Everyone should have a chance to let it weave its magic spell without thinking about how its effects were achieved or what was going on off-camera. After a showing, you can consult a variety of sources to learn about the unprecedented effort that went into its production as Metro-Goldwyn-Mayer (MGM) Studios' most expensive movie up to that time.

The film was not a smash hit when it was first released. It crept into the zeitgeist because of its annual airings on television. In the days long before cable TV, home video, or streaming, it could only be seen once a year on a broadcast network in prime time. Families circled the date on their calendars so as not to miss out. Anticipation was keen, to put it mildly.

My wife remembers watching the film on her family's black-and-white television set. It wasn't until the 1960s, with the growing popularity of color TV, that folks at home were finally able to appreciate one of the greatest moments in all of movie history: Dorothy's first sight of Oz. The transition from the humdrum, sepia-tinted Kansas world to the dazzling Technicolor land of Oz is unforgettable. Time hasn't dimmed the impact of this reveal, which we dare you to compare to any modern-day computer-generated effect. See if your family doesn't audibly react to this incredible moment.

The guardian of the gates in the Emerald City looks an awful lot like the man who drove Dorothy and her friends in his wagon . . . and also bears a striking resemblance to the Wizard himself. Frank Morgan plays all of those characters as well as Professor Marvel.

Every year a different star or group of stars was recruited to host the TV presentation, and for a time these introductory segments were produced and directed by Jack Haley Jr., whose father played the Tin Man. When I worked at *Entertainment Tonight*, I realized that no one had ever turned the camera on Jack, who visited the enormous set at MGM when he was a boy. So I did. His clearest memory was walking on the yellow brick road and bumping into a wall: the painted set created an illusion

Representatives of the Lollipop Guild offer a sample of their work to Dorothy. The three Munchkins are Harry Doll, Jerry Gerlich, and Jerry Maren.

for the viewer, but he confronted reality in that moment.

Judy Garland was never more endearing than she is in Oz. Her singing voice is so appealing that we may take her work as an actress for granted. If you and your family fall in love with Judy, the other film that's a must-see is *Meet Me in St. Louis* (1944), which is also covered in this book.

A quick trip to YouTube will enable you to enjoy performances, mostly from television variety shows, featuring Garland's talented costars Jack Haley, Bert Lahr, and Ray Bolger. If you tune in to Turner Classic Movies, you will have many opportunities to see Frank Morgan, Billie Burke, Margaret Hamilton, and the other players who were so well cast in this picture. See if your family can identify Morgan, who in addition to Professor Marvel appears briefly in three other roles. Subtle changes in his makeup may cast doubt that he's the same fellow—but he is.

Margaret Hamilton reveled in playing the Wicked Witch of the West and signed photographs to fellow cast members and fans alike "W.W.W.," which tells you a lot about her sense of humor. In real life, she was nothing like the villainess she plays so vividly. Everyone who met her held her in the highest regard. She even was a guest of Fred Rogers on *Mr. Rogers' Neighborhood* to prove she wasn't a real-life meanie. Following an appearance at the Telluride Film Festival in 1981, I witnessed flight staff tripping over themselves to take special care of her once they realized who she was.

A well-timed fire drill enabled me (Leonard) to meet another of Oz's leading lights at the Lincoln Center branch of the New York Public Library. I was taking a break from staring at old newspapers on a microfilm viewer when I realized that the man sitting right next to me was Jack Haley Sr. I managed to say hello but didn't want to disrupt him or anyone else. Just then a horn sounded loudly over the public-address system, and we were told to leave the building. I took advantage of this to ask Haley about his life and career, and he was happy to oblige as we

Dorothy and her new friends the Scarecrow, the Cowardly Lion, and the Tin Man have made their way to Oz. Now what's in store for them?

wandered over to the fountain plaza. He explained that he developed the voice of the Tin Man from reading stories to his son at bedtime in a breathless way. He demonstrated it for me, and it was as if thirty years melted away.

"Over the Rainbow" is the most famous song to emerge from the score but not the only piece of music commissioned for it. The suite of songs performed for Dorothy by the Munchkins represent a banquet of ingenuity: "Come Out, Come Out, Wherever You Are," "The House Began to Pitch," "As Mayor of the Munchkin City," "As Coroner, I Must Aver," "Ding Dong! The Witch Is Dead," "Lullaby League," "Lollipop Guild," and "We Welcome You to Munchkinland." You may think you know these songs, but their wordplay is so clever that you will find yourself discovering new delights upon each hearing. (If you've never heard Bobby McFerrin sing the entire medley a cappella, go look it up right now.) All hail E. Y. "Yip" Harburg and Harold Arlen for their wonderful words and music. They won an Oscar for "Over the Rainbow," and MGM workhorse Herbert Stothart earned another for his brilliant musical adaptation, including themes not connected with the songs that I, for one, have running through my head all the time.

The Wizard of Oz is eternal, and most attempts to copy it pale in comparison. The original is the one you want to share with your loved ones. Why? "Because, because, because, because, because!"

"Somewhere Over the Rainbow" Pizza

The Wizard himself would be impressed with this festive meal. If you're feeling ambitious, you can make the dough yourself—but a store-bought base works just fine. Same goes for your sauce. The focus on this pizza is bringing the rainbow to life, so let the ROYGBIV in your heart soar.

AMOUNT DEPENDS ON THE SIZE OF YOUR PIZZA

Cherry tomatoes, halved

Orange, green, red, and yellow bell peppers, sliced

Broccoli or broccolini, chopped

Red onion, sliced

Eggplant, chopped

Store-bought pizza dough

1 jar red pizza or pasta sauce

1 cup ricotta cheese

1 cup shredded mozzarella cheese

Balsamic glaze

Preheat your oven to 400°F before you start prepping your vegetables. This doesn't have to be a test of knife skills—and don't be embarrassed if that onion makes you cry.

Roll out your dough to the desired size. Carefully move the dough to a large sheet pan.

In a medium bowl, mix your red sauce and ricotta cheese together, then spread them over the pizza base, leaving space at the edges for the crust. Sprinkle a bit of mozzarella cheese on top.

Now is the fun part. Create your rainbow of vegetables. You can mix everything together or go by color, starting with your red cherry tomatoes, then your bell peppers. Next up is your green broccoli or broccolini, followed by your onions and eggplant.

You should now have a gorgeous rainbow in front of you. You can add more mozzarella cheese here or leave it as is. The final touch is drizzling some balsamic glaze on top of your creation.

Bake the pizza for about 18 minutes—a little longer if you like it crispy.

Pull out when finished and slice it up.

Velvet and the horse she falls in love with

NATIONAL VELVET

(1944)

123 MINUTES

Directed by Clarence Brown | **Produced by** Pandro S. Berman
Screenplay by Theodore Reeves and Helen Deutsch; based on the novel by Enid Bagnold | **Cinematography by** Leonard Smith | **Music by** Herbert Stothart
Cast: Mickey Rooney, Donald Crisp, Elizabeth Taylor, Anne Revere, Angela Lansbury, Jackie Jenkins, Juanita Quigley, Arthur Treacher, Reginald Owen, Norma Varden, Terry Kilburn, Arthur Shields, Dennis Hoey

It took almost a decade for Enid Bagnold's best-selling novel of 1935 to reach the screen, but it was well worth the wait. To have the masterful director Clarence Brown at the helm and a superb, handpicked cast filling every role would have been worth years more had it been necessary. In the main title sequence, a camera perches high over a country road, as a figure we recognize from behind as Mickey Rooney walks along, whistling. At the end of the credits, a title card sets the scene: "England in the late 1920s—a long time ago in a spinning world."

If your family only knows Angela Lansbury from her television series *Murder, She Wrote* or as the voice of Mrs. Potts in Disney's *Beauty and the Beast* (1991), you're in for a mild shock. The picture opens with schoolchildren bidding their teacher goodbye for the summer holiday, and Lansbury is revealed as one of the taller teenagers in the classroom. Velvet Brown (Elizabeth Taylor) is a bit awkward and shy—"she's always dreaming," her sister Malvolia remarks. She has three sisters and one baby brother (played by Jackie Jenkins, soon to earn the nickname "Butch"). Their father is the village butcher, who keeps his feelings in check except when gently prodded by his practical and all-knowing wife (Anne

Mr. Brown (Donald Crisp) and Mrs. Brown (Anne Revere) try to quell Velvet's (Elizabeth Taylor) excitement after the Grand National race. Mi (Mickey Rooney) has shorn her raven-colored hair.

Revere). When fourteen-year-old Velvet gets a glimpse of a neighbor's horse, Piebold, running wild and free, it's love at first sight. Through sheer luck she wins the horse in a town raffle. Then Velvet starts to dream big, determined that The Pie (as Piebold becomes known) can win the Grand National, the greatest racing event in all of England. When a drifter named Mi (Mickey Rooney) comes along and boards with the family, she finds an accomplice who knows about horses to help her realize her dream.

This is more than just the story of a girl and her infatuation with a magnificent animal. It is a portrait of a family, set in 1920s Sussex, a coastal town with spectacular views. Technicolor was invented for just such a setting.

Donald Crisp played more than his share of patriarchs on-screen and was familiar to moviegoers from such highly lauded films as John Ford's *How Green Was My Valley* (1941), which earned him an Academy Award. But the hot-tempered father who usually recognizes his own folly within minutes is a unique variation on that archetype. The screenplay for *National Velvet*, credited to Theodore Reeves and Helen Deutcsh, is disarmingly witty, imbuing Velvet's mother, beautifully underplayed by Anne Revere, with a rare wisdom that she's willing to share with her loving family. It seems that Mrs. Brown, the butcher's wife, had a dream of her own years ago: she swam the English Channel—and won one hundred gold sovereigns for it. She doesn't speak of those days very often but opens up to her adolescent daughter when the time is right. She also knows about the tumult that overnight fame can bring to an athlete and how to avoid those pitfalls.

Mickey Rooney was still entrenched in the role of all-American boy Andy Hardy from the famed film series he'd been starring in for the past seven years when this assignment came his way at MGM. Having given an Oscar-nominated performance in *The Human Comedy* (1943) the year before, he impressed director Clarence Brown, who had directed everyone from Greta Garbo to John Barrymore. Why? As he told film scholar Scott Eyman,

> Mickey Rooney is the closest thing to a genius that I ever worked with. There was Chaplin, then there was Rooney. That little bastard could do no wrong in my book. I don't know how he did it, because he never really paid any attention. Between takes he'd be off somewhere calling his bookmaker, then come back and go into a scene as if he'd been rehearsing for three days.
>
> The scene [in *The Human Comedy*] where he reads the telegram announcing his brother's death—we must have shot that thing four or five times, and each time he'd read it as though he'd seen it for the first time. All you had to do was rehearse it once. You know the scene where he runs the hurdles? Well, he'd never hurdled in his life before that; he tried it four or five times and said, "I'm ready, Boss," and when we shot it, he beat high school kids, with no faking, who had done it all their lives.

Look at the size of those lights—and how close they are to Elizabeth Taylor and Mickey Rooney. The Technicolor camera is also quite large. All this for a "simple" shot of the two actors driving a horse cart.

Yet here he was again, playing a young man—not a kid, but still a very young man—just weeks before the draft board conscripted him into the United States Army.

This film also offered young Elizabeth Taylor a signature role that she clung to for many years. In 1989, she told me (Leonard) that she didn't feel that she was acting at all in the film but merely playing herself. In the years to come, she developed skills that set her apart from other famous beauties and earned a well-deserved Academy Award for her performance as Martha in *Who's Afraid of Virginia Woolf?* (1966), an adaptation of the Edward Albee play that we don't recommend as family fodder.

Her memories of making *National Velvet* were vivid even when I spoke to her in 1989. As it happens, the book the movie was based on was one of the young actress's favorites. "As a child, that was a great experience for me because [the character] was an extension of myself. It was just kind of being me, and I even chose the horse. The studio gave me the horse, and I had him until he died. I was twelve and it was just like being told to live your fantasy . . . play for several months at the thing you liked best." But acting the part also meant allowing Mickey Rooney to shear off her long hair right on camera—there were no tricks to hide it. Would any of the adolescents in your family allow such a thing to happen? What if it meant you could live out your dreams in return?

In 1960 MGM produced a TV series based on the book and movie. Young Lori Martin won the role of Velvet, and the series ran for two years. That was a better outcome than they had when, in search of a star vehicle for recent Oscar-winner Tatum O'Neal, they devised a theatrical feature called *International Velvet* (1978). Comparisons to the original film were inevitable, and the odds were in the 1944 movie's favor.

Despite changing attitudes toward women in sports—and in society—*National Velvet* holds up quite well. It is definitely of its period and takes place in an even earlier part of the twentieth century, but the emotions it conveys are ageless.

National Velvet
Carrot Cake Cupcakes

Horses love their carrots, and so will you. Let's jump into the saddle and make some carrot cake cupcakes.

MAKES 6 STANDARD CUPCAKES, OR 12 MINIS

FOR THE CUPCAKES:

Nonstick cooking spray or butter

1¼ cups vegetable oil

1 cup granulated sugar

1 cup brown sugar

1 teaspoon vanilla extract

1 small banana, mashed

3 large eggs

2 cups all-purpose flour

2 teaspoons baking soda

1½ teaspoons cinnamon

¼ teaspoon ground cloves

¼ teaspoon ground ginger

½ teaspoon sea salt

½ cup chopped walnuts

½ cup chopped pecans

½ cup brown raisins

4 to 6 medium carrots, grated (about 3 cups)

FOR THE CREAM CHEESE FROSTING:

8 ounces cream cheese, softened (a brick works best)

½ cup (1 stick) unsalted butter, at room temperature

1 teaspoon vanilla extract

½ teaspoon kosher salt

¼ teaspoon nutmeg

1¼ cups confectioners' sugar

Preheat the oven to 350°F. Grease a muffin tin with nonstick cooking spray or butter, or insert cupcake liners. In a large bowl, whisk the vegetable oil, granulated sugar, brown sugar, and vanilla. Slowly whisk in your mashed banana, then slowly whisk in your eggs one by one. Set aside.

In a separate bowl, whisk the flour, baking soda, cinnamon, cloves, ginger, and salt.

Combine the contents of the two bowls, using a a spatula to gently fold ingredients together until smooth. Add the nuts, raisins, and grated carrots, and gently stir until smooth.

Spoon the mixture into your cupcake molds, filling each about halfway. Bake for 20 minutes.

While the cupcakes are baking, make the frosting. In a large bowl, combine your cream cheese and butter using an electric mixer. When it looks creamy, begin adding in the vanilla, salt, and nutmeg. Lastly, slowly add in the confectioners' sugar. When everything is combined and lump-free, it's ready.

After 20 minutes in the oven, check on your cupcakes using a toothpick. When the toothpick comes out clean, they are ready to go. Let them cool to room temperature before adding your frosting with a knife, spoon, or piping bag. Add a nut or two on top for a little panache.

Margaret O'Brien as Tootie and Judy Garland as her big sister Esther, who is about to sing "Have Yourself a Merry Little Christmas"

MEET ME IN ST. LOUIS

(1944)

113 MINUTES

Directed by Vincente Minnelli | **Produced by** Arthur Freed
Screenplay by Irving Brecher and Fred F. Finklehoffe; based on short stories by Sally Benson | **Musical direction by** George Stoll | **Songs by** Hugh Martin and Ralph Blane | **Cast:** Judy Garland, Margaret O'Brien, Mary Astor, Lucille Bremer, Leon Ames, Tom Drake, Marjorie Main, Harry Davenport, June Lockhart, Henry H. Daniels Jr., Joan Carroll, Hugh Marlowe, Robert Sally, Chill Wills

What a wonderful movie this is—the kind you can watch endless times and never tire of it. The music is ageless, and the world it depicts is the kind you wish you were part of. It's 1903, and all of St. Louis is giddy with excitement over the imminent opening of the city's centennial Louisiana Purchase Exposition, also known as the St. Louis World's Fair. A song has been written called "Meet Me in St. Louis," and everybody is singing it . . . especially in the Smith household.

Breadwinner Alonzo Smith (Leon Ames) arrives home after a hard day's work wanting nothing more than a soak in the tub and a quiet dinner prepared by housekeeper Katie (Marjorie Main). He has no inkling that his family is planning to dine an hour early so the eldest, Rose (Lucille Bremer), can accept a long-distance phone call from her boyfriend, who might just offer a marriage proposal. Landing a husband is the ultimate goal of almost every young woman, and she needs privacy to have that conversation. Everyone is in on the plan except Alonzo, who isn't willing to sacrifice his soak or alter his schedule. That's how we meet the members of this loving clan. The rest of the film isn't so much a linear story as a series of charming

Leon Ames tries to lay down the law to the women in his family: Lucille Bremer, Mary Astor (seated), and Judy Garland.

vignettes involving trolley rides, parties, and the possibility of moving away.

That's the world that Sally Benson experienced as a young girl in St. Louis and evoked so vividly in a series of stories first published in *The New Yorker* magazine under the title "5135 Kensington Avenue." She later compiled these stories into a book, *Meet Me in St. Louis*. MGM purchased the film rights and hired Benson to write the screenplay. While she was on the payroll, art-director-turned-movie-director Vincente Minnelli had her describe in detail what her three-story house looked like and how it was decorated.

The resulting movie is one people have loved and cherished for the past eighty years. The idealized family it depicts is one we hold dear. Leon Ames plays the father, Mary Astor is his loving wife, Judy Garland is their teenaged daughter, and Margaret O'Brien is their youngest child with the wildest imagination. Harry Davenport is the kind of grandfather we all wish we had, and Marjorie Main is officially a servant but in truth the empress of her kitchen domain.

As Dorothy in *The Wizard of Oz*, Judy Garland was a winsome adolescent. In *Meet Me in St. Louis*, she is embracing the first taste of womanhood and she looks especially beautiful. There are a couple of reasons for this: a new makeup artist took her on at the studio, and director Vincente Minnelli was falling in love with her; as a result, she is positively luminous. They married the year after the film was released and had a baby daughter one year later. She is Liza Minnelli, the offspring of two prodigiously talented people.

Songwriters Hugh Martin and Ralph Blane were relative newcomers to Hollywood, recruited after the success of a show called *Best Foot Forward*. They were tasked with providing a handful of songs for Judy Garland and the irrepressible Margaret O'Brien. The number they perform together for their party guests, "Under the Bamboo Tree," was a novelty

Tom Drake, as the boy next door, calls on Judy Garland, under the watchful eye of her sister, Lucille Bremer.

hit from 1902. The sentimental song that Mary Astor and Leon Ames sing to affirm their love and devotion, "You and I," was written by Martin and Blane for that particular moment in the script. Producer Arthur Freed dubbed Ames's voice himself, but you'd never know it.

The showpieces are songs that became a permanent part of Judy Garland's repertoire: "The Trolley Song," "The Boy Next Door," and the evergreen "Have Yourself a Merry Little Christmas."

The eye for detail that became a hallmark of director Minnelli's work was fully realized in this handsome Technicolor production. The story takes place over the course of a year. Because it includes a Christmas celebration, it has become a holiday perennial on television. But there is much to savor year-round in this beautifully crafted film.

Margaret O'Brien is perfect as the mischievous Tootie, who possesses a wild and unexpectedly dark imagination. At age seven, she was a major star and was presented with a Academy Juvenile Award for her work in 1944. She has nothing but positive memories of working with Garland.

If your family isn't familiar with period pieces from the turn of the last century, you might discuss what the most striking difference is between then and now—aside from the introduction of television, cellular phones, and the internet. And say, whatever happened to deliveries of ice from horse-drawn wagons like the one operated by Chill Wills at the beginning of this movie?

Hickory Nut Cake

Save some starch from your collar and throw it into this wonderful old recipe. Maybe even share some penuche frosting on the trolley.

MAKES 1 9-INCH CAKE

FOR THE CAKE:

⅔ cup (1⅓ sticks) unsalted butter, at room temperature

2 cups granulated sugar

3 large eggs, at room temperature

1 teaspoon vanilla extract

1 cup whole milk

2½ cups all-purpose flour

2 teaspoons baking powder

½ teaspoon nutmeg

½ teaspoon cinnamon

⅛ teaspoon kosher salt

Nonstick cooking spray or butter

1 cup chopped hickory nuts (or pecans)

FOR THE PENUCHE FROSTING:

½ cup butter

1 cup brown sugar

¼ cup 2% milk, gently warmed on the stove for a minute

1 cup confectioners' sugar

Preheat your oven to 325°F.

Start with the cake. In a large bowl, use an electric mixer to combine the butter and sugar. Add in one egg and mix well. Repeat for each egg, and then the vanilla. Pour in milk. Set aside.

In a medium bowl, combine the flour, baking powder, nutmeg, cinnamon, and salt. Using the electric mixer, slowly begin incorporating the dry ingredients into the wet ingredients, beating well.

Grease a 9-inch pan with nonstick cooking spray or butter. Pour the batter into the pan and bake for 25 minutes.

While the cake is baking, make the frosting. Melt the butter in a small saucepan over medium-low heat, then add in your brown sugar and bring to a boil. Wait until the mixture thickens, then slowly stir in the warm milk. Begin slowly stirring in the confectioners' sugar until the consistency is thin and good for spreading.

Let the cake cool to room temperature, then cover it with frosting and sprinkle hickory nuts on top.

Katie Nolan (Dorothy McGuire) works her fingers to the bone for her children, Francie (Peggy Ann Garner) and Cornelius (Ted Donaldson).

A TREE GROWS IN BROOKLYN

(1945)

129 MINUTES

Directed by Elia Kazan | **Produced by** Louis D. Lighton
Cinematography by Leon Shamroy | **Music by** Alfred Newman
Costumes by Bonnie Cashin | **Cast:** Dorothy McGuire, Peggy Ann Garner, Joan Blondell, James Dunn, Lloyd Nolan, James Gleason, Ted Donaldson, Ruth Nelson, John Alexander, B. S. Pully, Charles Halton, J. Farrell MacDonald, Erskine Sanford, Art Smith, Adeline de Walt Reynolds

Not all great family films are filled with sunshine and light. Walt Disney, for one, believed that in order to appreciate those qualities, an audience had to go through darkness first. That's why so many of the selections in this book have elements of drama or loss; leading characters must *earn* their happy ending, and so do we in the audience. Sometimes this involves having what used to be known as "a good cry." Some family members may find it difficult to keep their emotions in check, so for this film in particular, have a box of tissues handy.

A Tree Grows in Brooklyn breaks your heart not once but multiple times on its winding road to a cathartic finale. It is, in every sense, a beautiful movie, and it marked the Hollywood debut for legendary director Elia Kazan.

He called his young star Peggy Ann Garner a "miracle." She inhabits the role of Francie Nolan completely. Francie and her brother live with their mother and father in a dingy tenement flat in 1912 Brooklyn, New York. When a city crew cuts down a shady tree right outside their window, Francie despairs, but her ever-optimistic

Father and daughter have a special connection in *A Tree Grows in Brooklyn.* Both James Dunn and Peggy Ann Garner won Academy Awards.

father says that it will be replaced, because a tree, like sprigs of grass, will find a way to burst through cracks in the sidewalk. Francie's mother works nonstop, scrubbing floors and piling up rags for her children to sell to a local scrap dealer. She counts every penny and doesn't let one cent go to waste. Her sociable sister Sissy (Joan Blondell) scolds her for growing colder and colder, "hard inside," while her ne'er-do-well husband earns an occasional living as a singing waiter, when he's sober. He and Francie have a deep connection, and he arranges for her to go to a school outside their neighborhood where she can get a better education and pursue her love of writing. All Francie's mother can see is that it will drain the family treasury.

Elia Kazan had made some documentaries, but this was his first endeavor in Hollywood, under the watchful eye of 20th Century Fox chief Darryl F. Zanuck. He later wrote,

> Our story was based on a complex character, a man who was a drunk and a dissembler, a failure but still charming, able to hold the true and lasting love of his young daughter. It was a part that might have been acted on stage. For the screen, however, it seemed to Bud [Louis Lighton, the producer] and to me that we had to look for and find a man who was a failure but still charming; a drunk, reformed or persisting; a dissembler who was nevertheless lovable. So we looked for such a man who happened to be an actor. And we did a piece of casting that seemed like a miracle: Jimmy Dunn. I knew what I had in Jimmy before I started photographing him, and so did Bud. Here was an actor who once had great promise. It was generally believed that nothing would prevent him from becoming a big star—except what

Joan Blondell, as Aunt Sissy, injects life and a bit of irreverence into the proceedings whenever she stops by the family apartment.

> did, his drinking. In casting files, he was marked: 'Drinks!' That got around. He didn't get parts. This cracked his ego. He felt guilty of self-betrayal. I could see that on his face the first time I talked to him. That was what I would photograph—that face in stress.

Dunn has the most poignant scene in the picture when he sits at a piano to sing and play the old Scottish ballad "Annie Laurie." I can't hear that melancholy song without remembering its effect in this movie.

The director, who would soon return to New York and revolutionize the world of theater in general and acting in particular (in tandem with Marlon Brando) believed that "You can't get it out of them unless it's in 'em" and took a psychological approach to each performer in this ensemble piece. Every role, no matter how small, is perfectly realized, from Lloyd Nolan as the good-

Lloyd Nolan, as the Irish cop on the beat, treats James Dunn with kid gloves even when he's "in his cups."

hearted neighborhood cop to B. S. Pully, who sells Christmas trees and throws the leftovers into the waiting arms of would-be young customers as Christmas Eve comes to a close.

On-screen, the movie bears the official title *Betty Smith's A Tree Grows in Brooklyn*, as her 1943 novel was a runaway bestseller and there was a ready-made audience for the film. It maintained the essence of the book while compressing events and eliminating some characters. Credit the husband-and-wife team of Tess Slesinger and Frank Davis for their exceptional, Oscar-nominated screenplay. (Sad to say, Slesinger died of cancer shortly after the film's release.)

More than once, Francie is told to say what's on her mind clearly instead of indirectly, but that's part of her character makeup. She takes in the world around her with a sense of wonder and possibility. Her schoolteacher (Ruth Nelson) recognizes and admires this quality and encourages her to write about what she knows. Peggy Ann Garner embodies these traits and understandably earned an Academy Juvenile Award for her performance. It was the highlight of an abbreviated film career. James Dunn's portrayal of her loving father won over Academy members who voted him Best Supporting Actor of 1945.

Toward the end of the film, Francie wonders aloud why people only show their kindness and compassion at Christmastime and wishes it could be that way all year. Don't we all?

Brooklyn Corned Beef and Cabbage

Most of us yearn for something more in our lives—but sometimes comfort food is exactly what you need. Old-fashioned corned beef and cabbage can really hit the spot.

MAKES 4 SERVINGS

2 pounds corned beef brisket

½ garlic clove, minced

2 russet potatoes, quartered

4 small red potatoes, quartered

2 large carrots, chopped

1 medium sweet onion, chopped

1 teaspoon yellow mustard

2 bay leaves

½ cup (1 stick) unsalted butter

1 medium head cabbage, quartered

Fresh parsley, for garnish

Place the corned beef in a Dutch oven or large pot. Fill the pot with water so it just barely covers the top of the beef. Bring the pot to a boil, then reduce heat and simmer until tender, about 2 to 3 hours (or 1 hour per pound of meat).

When your beef is tender, add the garlic, potatoes, carrots, and onion to the pot. Bring to a boil again, then let simmer for another 10 minutes.

Add the mustard, bay leaves, butter, and cabbage to the pot. Repeat the step above.

Remove the bay leaves, then transfer the food from your pot to a platter. Let the meat rest for 10 minutes before slicing. Garnish with parsley and use your broth as a perfect au jus.

Donald O'Connor and Gene Kelly are airborne at this point in the "Moses Supposes" number.

SINGIN' IN THE RAIN

(1952)

103 MINUTES

Directed by Gene Kelly and Stanley Donen | **Produced by** Arthur Freed
Screenplay by Betty Comden and Adolph Green | **Cinematography by** Harold Rosson
Art direction by Cedric Gibbons and Randall Duell | **Musical direction by** Lennie Hayton
Songs by Arthur Freed and Nacio Herb Brown | **Cast:** Gene Kelly, Donald O'Connor, Debbie Reynolds, Jean Hagen, Millard Mitchell, Cyd Charisse, Douglas Fowley, Rita Moreno, Madge Blake, King Donovan, Kathleen Freeman, Julius Tannen, Paul Maxey, Dawn Addams, Mae Clarke, Joi Lansing, Ray McDonald, William Schallert, Snub Pollard, Bobby Watson

We know that not everybody loves musicals, but there's a reason that so many people name this as the best one ever made. The comedy component is just as potent as the sensational singing and dancing. Its showpiece numbers stand on their own, even without the context of the clever story.

The story is told in flashback as movie star Don Lockwood (Gene Kelly) is interviewed at the Hollywood premiere of his latest picture, in which he stars with perpetual leading lady Lina Lamont (Jean Hagen). His lifelong pal Cosmo Brown (Donald O'Connor) is also on hand. The romantic stars pose happily together, but the truth is that Don can't stand Lina, who has the high-pitched, grating voice of a Brooklyn cab driver. Later that night, Don chances to meet a young performer named Cathy Selden (Debbie Reynolds), who is part of the entertainment at a fancy party. At the studio the next day, Don learns that Cathy's promising career has been sabotaged—by a vindictive Lina. Meanwhile, *The Jazz Singer* opens and creates an overnight demand for talkies. A long night of brainstorming brings Don, Cathy, and Cosmo a perfect solution: transform their silent film *The*

This shot appears at the very beginning of the film as part of the main title sequence, but it captures the wonderful spirit of the picture.

Dueling Cavalier into *The Dancing Cavalier* by adding musical numbers. The only problem is Lina's squeaky voice. Cosmo shows his pals how to fix that by substituting Cathy's voice on the soundtrack. At the premiere, studio boss R. F. Simpson is backed into a corner by Lina, who threatens to sue him if the truth comes out.

Singin' in the Rain was written by Betty Comden and Adolph Green, whose Broadway hit *On the Town* (in which they also starred) was their ticket to Hollywood. But producer Arthur Freed never let them show their faces on camera. Instead, he kept them busy writing screenplays—for *Good News* (1947), *On the Town* (1949), and *The Band Wagon* (1953), all of which are also family favorites that we recommend—and this gem came with an imperative: craft a story that would include an array of vintage hit songs, written years ago by the very same Arthur Freed, in partnership with lyricist Nacio Herb Brown.

They reasoned that since the songs were introduced in the late 1920s and 1930s, the film should take place in that time period: the end of the silent era and the beginning of talkies. Once they cracked that challenge, everything else fell

He's singin' and dancin' in the rain.

into place, bit by bit. The corniest of the old songs ("Wedding of the Painted Doll," "Beautiful Girl") were treated in a satiric fashion, while the numbers that held up by modern standards ("You Were Meant for Me," "Good Morning") were given more TLC. Buoyed by the reception to the previous year's Oscar-winning *An American in Paris* (with its seventeen-minute ballet finale), directors Gene Kelly and Stanley Donen concocted another "dream ballet" to serve as the climax of this film. It was inspired by the Freed–Brown hit "Broadway Melody," the title song of the 1929 release that went on to win Best Picture at the Academy Awards.

If your family isn't familiar with this form of dance and thinks of ballet in a classical form, you can tell them that a choreographer named Agnes de Mille pioneered the use of dance to tell a story in the landmark Broadway show *Oklahoma!* She even had dancers step into the roles of the actors who were playing the leading characters in the play. Had she not done that successfully, Gene Kelly wouldn't have been free to create the "Broadway Melody" sequence, which tells a story about a young man who's "gotta dance" and shows up in New York to do just that. The dreamy quality of the pantomime story is enhanced by a dream-within-a-dream, in which our young hero meets a femme fatale, played by the bewitching dancing star Cyd Charisse. This interruption to the story came as an unwelcome surprise to Jessie when she first watched the movie. This is the one component of the film that may or may not hold your family's interest.

That isn't the only imaginative use of dance in this exceptional film. Gene Kelly, feeling giddy at having spent quality time with Debbie Reynolds, can only express how he feels by dancing, even though the skies have opened up and it's pouring outside. (We recommend putting our book down and returning after you've seen the movie because we're now going to discuss how some key scenes were created.) Kelly and his directing partner, Stanley Donen, planned every single step of the "Singin' in the Rain" number and could tell the crew where to dig holes for puddles and where to leave the sidewalk free of obstacles. It was actually shot in broad daylight with a black tarpaulin covering the set at MGM Studios in Culver City, California. That's movie magic at work.

Debbie Reynolds was still a newcomer when she was selected to play the role of Cathy Selden. Rehearsing with Kelly and Donald O'Connor for the "Good Morning" number tested her mettle, and she never forgot how her feet were bleeding at the end of the workday. But success in show

Donald O'Connor, Debbie Reynolds, and Gene Kelly sing "Good Morning."

business means never losing that smile when you're entertaining an audience, and Debbie understood that.

Donald O'Connor grew up in his family's vaudeville act but had to "up his game" working in tandem with Gene Kelly, even though they make it look easy when they perform "Fit as a Fiddle" and "Moses Supposes."

The one new song written expressly for this film is "Make 'em Laugh," which came about when O'Connor was fooling around at lunchtime one day. His spontaneous antics inspired Kelly to formalize his routine and create an unforgettable performance, arguably the funniest musical number ever put on film. The song, penned by Arthur Freed and Nacio Herb Brown, was strikingly similar to Cole Porter's "Be a Clown," which he wrote for producer Freed's 1948 movie *The Pirate*, in which Gene Kelly starred. Mr. Porter was not amused by the resemblance but took no legal action.

There are three women who deserve to be singled out for attention along with Debbie Reynolds. First is Jean Hagen, who is so good as Lina Lamont that she earned an Academy Award nomination as Best Supporting Actress. (She lost to Gloria Grahame in another tale of Hollywood, 1952's *The Bad and the Beautiful*.) Unfortunately, she was so convincing playing a so-called dumb blonde that producers couldn't picture her in any other kind of part, so she never enjoyed the career boost that an Oscar nomination often brings. In the tiny part of Zelda, who rats out Cathy Selden, is a very young Rita Moreno, who would go on to win an Academy Award for *West Side Story* (1961). And in the role of self-serious speech coach Phoebe Dinsmore, twenty-nine-year-old Kathleen Freeman made her mark at the outset of a long career in comedy. She was a particular favorite of Jerry Lewis and, in later years, director John Landis.

They met on Broadway and scored in Hollywood: codirectors Gene Kelly and Stanley Donen.

Watching this film makes you want to get up and dance.

"Good Morning" Breakfast for Dinner

One of the best numbers in the film has inspired us to eat breakfast for dinner. Let's have some sunny-side-up eggs and bacon. You can even make them into a smiley face.

MAKES 4 SERVINGS

1 package of center cut bacon

8 slices of sourdough bread

Butter, for toast

Olive oil for cooking

8 large eggs

Kosher salt and freshly ground black pepper

Add the bacon strips to a large cold skillet and turn the heat up to medium. Sauté, flipping the strips often to promote even browning, until you've reached your desired doneness. (We're a crispy bacon household—Alice Maltin takes this very seriously—but you are welcome to serve it how you like.) Remove the bacon from the skillet and place it on a paper towel to absorb excess grease.

For the toast, you can use a whole sourdough loaf or one that is pre-sliced. Toast your slices up and spread with butter (real butter—let's just go for it and leave the substitutes behind).

Finally, let's make sunny-side-up eggs. It may seem daunting, but we promise you can do it. Heat olive oil in the skillet over medium heat for about 3 minutes. (Alternately, use the leftover bacon grease.) Gently crack 4 eggs one by one over the skillet. Cover the skillet with a lid and let the eggs cook for 2 minutes; the whites should be hardening but not the yolk. Remove the lid and carefully slide the eggs off your skillet and onto a plate and season to taste. Repeat with the 4 remaining eggs.

Add fruit and vegetables if you like, but remember—it's the simple things. Fresh ingredients, your family, and one of the greatest musical movies of all time.

The makings of a love triangle: Doris Day is flanked by Philip Carey and Howard Keel.

CALAMITY JANE

(1953)

101 MINUTES

Directed by David Butler | **Produced by** William Jacobs
Screenplay by James O'Hanlon | **Cinematography by** Wilfrid M. Cline
Musical numbers staged by Jack Donohue | **Musical direction by** Ray Heindorf
Songs by Sammy Fain and Paul Francis Webster | **Cast:** Doris Day, Howard Keel, Allyn Ann McLerie, Philip Carey, Dick Wesson, Paul Harvey, Chubby Johnson, Gale Robbins, I. Stanford Jolley, Rex Lease, Jimmy Lloyd, Pierce Lyden, Emmett Lynn, Chuck Roberson, Glenn Strange

For moviegoers, it was love at first sight with Doris Day. She made her debut in 1949's *Romance on the High Seas*, and four years later she headlined this boisterous movie musical and made the title role her own. What's more, one of its original songs, "Secret Love," became a massive hit. Doris could do no wrong.

Calamity Jane and Bill Hickok were real people, but you'd never guess it from watching this movie in which they are played larger than life. I first showed *Calamity Jane* to my young daughter because a) it's about a tomboy, which I thought would amuse her, and b) she already recognized Doris Day from *The Pajama Game* and Howard Keel from *Seven Brides for Seven Brothers*. (We all love musicals in this family.)

Those remain valid reasons to watch this Hollywood original, obviously inspired by the great success of the Broadway play and movie *Annie Get Your Gun*, which MGM had filmed to great success in 1950. Warner Bros. even hired that film's leading man, Howard Keel, who played a similar character opposite Betty Hutton as sharpshooter Annie Oakley.

Calamity Jane has one of the most dynamic openings of any musical ever

Calamity Jane breaks into the dressing room of a stage star, Adelaid Adams (Gale Robbins), in Chicago.

made. We meet the title character singing a lively song about the Deadwood Stage out loud, perched atop a stagecoach pulled by six horses, racing at a furious pace. When she disembarks in Deadwood City, she never stops warbling and segues into the next song, "Introducing Henry Miller." Whew! What a ride, and what a great way to establish the time period (the 1870s) and introduce us to the Golden Garter saloon. The musical numbers were staged and directed by stage and screen veteran Jack Donohue.

Calamity (or Calam, as everyone calls her) considers Wild Bill Hickok her best friend, but she has a serious crush on tall, handsome Lieutenant Dan Gilmartin of the US Army. She even sneaks into Sioux territory and rescues him from the warlike tribe. (This was made at the height of Hollywood's unenlightened depiction of Native Americans.) Bill genuinely likes Calam but mentions, more than once, that he wouldn't mind seeing her looking more ladylike, fixing her hair, applying makeup, and wearing a dress. Calam, who wears an old US Army cap and a soldier's dirty uniform (with a holster for her pistol) pays no attention. When the owner of the Golden Garter fails to bring fabled

Calamity Jane (Doris Day) cheers on her accidental discovery, Katie Brown (Allyn Ann McLerie).

entertainer Adelaid Adams to town, Calam takes on the job herself. In Chicago, she barges into Adams's dressing room just as her maid is posing in one of the star's revealing outfits and mistakes her for Adelaid. A short time later, when Katie Brown admits to her hard-bitten Deadwood audience that she isn't Adelaid after all, it's Calamity who speaks up on her behalf, and a friendship is sealed. That is, until Lieutenant Gilmartin develops feelings for Katie—and Calamity realizes that it's time to show her feminine side to the world.

Doris Day was still a relative newcomer to movies, but she endeared herself to audiences overnight and was well cast with Gordon MacRae in such lighthearted musicals as *Tea for Two* (1950), *On Moonlight Bay* (1951), and *By the Light of the Silvery Moon* (1953). She even acquitted herself nicely in a dramatic role in the underrated *Storm Warning* (1950). Warner Bros. was always on the lookout for the right kind of material to showcase their singing star, and *Calamity Jane*, written by James O'Hanlon (whose brother George headlined the studio's *Joe McDoakes* comedy shorts) filled the bill to perfection. The musical numbers were staged by show-business veteran Jack Donohue.

Speaking of veterans, David Butler, who made four of Shirley Temple's biggest hits in the 1930s and the first of the wacky *Road* pictures with Bob Hope and Bing Crosby, knew that the rip-snorting character of Calamity Jane and her on-again, off-again pal Wild Bill Hickok would have to be played for laughs, so all the performances are broad and unsubtle. As is the message of the story: be a tomboy all you like, but when you want to attract attention from a man, it's easier if you dress nicely and look your best. This being the 1950s, there was no irony intended in any of this. Women were expected to clean house and keep the fires burning (unlike Day, who off-screen was pursuing a career while raising a son, Terry Melcher).

Howard Keel was what we call today "the whole package," almost too good to be true: a fine figure of a man with a glorious singing voice who made everything he did seem effortless. Yet even he must have winced when he saw the setup of the song "I Can Do Without You," which is a transparent paraphrase of the great Irving Berlin song "Anything You Can Do" from *Annie Get Your Gun*.

The supporting roles are filled by Broadway transplant Allyn Ann McLerie, Warner Bros. contract comedian Dick Wesson, and up-and-coming actor Philip Carey. The enormous saloon set is jampacked with familiar faces from dozens of Western movies and television shows.

Composer Sammy Fain and lyricist Paul Francis Webster provided eleven songs altogether, including the rousing "The Deadwood Stage (Whip-Crack-Away)" and the musical's breakout hit, "Secret Love." It's no secret that this was destined to outlive the film. When "Secret Love" was released as a single shortly before the movie debuted, it stayed on the Billboard chart for twenty-two weeks, landing in the number one position four weeks in a row.

As for the movie, it's still what it always intended to be: pure fun. When you become a parent, you are suddenly much more aware of gender stereotypes and how your kids are going to feel when they see certain character portrayals. We can't change history, but we can meet it on its own terms.

The sheet music for "Secret Love" is a virtual poster for *Calamity Jane.*

Calam's Biscuits

Good old-fashioned biscuits and bacon jam—even Wild Bill himself can't resist these, and there's nothing secret about this love.

MAKES 8 BISCUITS

FOR THE BACON JAM:

1 pound center-cut bacon (cured or uncured)

1 large yellow onion, chopped

1 garlic clove, minced

¼ cup maple syrup

⅓ cup balsamic vinegar

⅓ cup brown sugar

FOR THE BISCUITS:

2 cups all-purpose flour

1 teaspoon baking powder

1 teaspoon garlic powder

½ teaspoon onion powder

1 teaspoon granulated sugar

½ teaspoon kosher salt

½ cup (1 stick) salted butter, melted

1 cup whole milk

½ cup shredded cheddar cheese

½ cup shredded Gruyère cheese

Make the bacon jam. Start by cooking the bacon in a large skillet (see recipe on page 59); fry until crispy. Remove the bacon from the skillet and transfer to a plate. When it's cool enough to handle, begin crumbling up the bacon with your hands. Pour out most of the bacon grease from your skillet, leaving just a small amount to cook with.

Turn the heat back up to medium and add the onion and garlic to the skillet. Sauté until golden. Stir in the maple syrup, balsamic vinegar, and brown sugar and bring to a boil. Once boiling, stir in the crumbled bacon pieces, then reduce heat to low. Cook uncovered, stirring intermittently for about 1 hour, then remove from heat.

You can serve the jam as is or put it in a blender or food processor for a few minutes, depending on how thick you want it to be.

Make the biscuits next. Preheat the oven to 425°F and line a baking sheet with parchment paper.

In a large bowl, combine the flour, baking powder, garlic powder, onion powder, sugar, and salt. Add the melted butter and milk to the bowl and stir to combine, then fold in the shredded cheese.

Begin to create small balls of dough with your hands and spread them out evenly on your sheet pan. If desired, brush a little melted butter on top before putting the biscuits in the oven. Bake for 12 minutes, or until golden brown.

Serve warm with the jam.

Milly's (Jane Powell) first encounter with her new brothers-in-law.

SEVEN BRIDES FOR SEVEN BROTHERS

(1954)

102 MINUTES

Directed by Stanley Donen | **Produced by** Jack Cummings
Screenplay by Albert Hackett, Frances Goodrich, Dorothy Kingsley; based on "The Sobbin' Women" by Stephen Vincent Benét
Music supervision by Saul Chaplin | **Musical direction by** Adolph Deutsch
Songs by Johnny Mercer and Gene DePaul | **Photographed by** George Folsey
Cast: Howard Keel, Jane Powell, Russ Tamblyn, Jeff Richards, Tommy Rall, Marc Platt, Matt Mattox, Jacques d'Amboise, Julie Newmar, Nancy Kilgas, Betty Carr, Virginia Gibson, Ruta Kilmonis (Lee), Norma Doggett, Ian Wolfe, Howard Petrie, Russell Simpson

As we shared in the introduction to this book, when Jessie was three years old, we showed her the barn-raising sequence in *Seven Brides for Seven Brothers*, and she was immediately hooked by the music and dancing. Then, after several weeks, she became curious about the characters, especially Russ Tamblyn, and we showed her the entire picture. Today, more than thirty-five years later, it remains her all-time favorite movie.

Whatever your age, you can't watch *Seven Brides for Seven Brothers* without shaking your head in wonderment. Here are virile, athletic men turning what is essentially a lumberyard into a dance stage. Do you still think dancing is for "sissies"? Think again . . . and watch *Seven Brides*.

The challenge for choreographer Michael Kidd was how to create a collage of dance movement for his manly cast members. He let his imagination run free,

The barn dance starts off innocently enough . . . but stand back!

as we see in the finished work: a two-by-four becomes a narrow trampoline, an axe becomes a prop, and a foundation floor is suddenly alive with backwoods mountain men who steal the local ladies' hearts right in front of their rivals' eyes.

The word *jubilant* seems to have been invented to describe *Seven Brides for Seven Brothers.* Designed to fill the new wide, rectangular screens most theaters had installed by 1954, it was never possible to appreciate the choreography at home until TV sets also went wide in the early part of the twenty-first century. Just to be safe, MGM had director Stanley Donen shoot every scene twice, once in the new CinemaScope process and once in the conventional 1.33:1 format. (When I spoke to him decades later, Jacques D'Amboise had a dim memory of his director saying "OK, everybody move closer together" when it came time to shoot the "flat" version.) That meant there were two editing rooms working on the picture simultaneously.

Seven Brides is based on Stephen Vincent Benét's short story "The Sobbin' Women," which in turn is based on a Roman myth about the Sabine women that has inspired painters for centuries. Transplanted to 1870, the movie opens with big, burly Adam Pontipee (Howard Keel) coming to town from his remote mountain home to get a shave and a haircut, along with some supplies . . . and to find himself a wife. When he sees how

The rivalry is out in the open now: the Pontipee brothers versus the townspeople.

pretty Milly (Jane Powell) stands up for herself while feeding customers at a local beanery, he figures she's the right woman for him. It's love at first sight, and against her better judgment, she agrees to marry him and accompany him back to the mountains, little dreaming what waits for her: six rambunctious brothers and a house that's never been swept clean. She soon tames the siblings by shaving and bathing them and tries to teach them some manners—even how to dance. The newly "civilized" family attends a barn-raising, but when the boys approach the pretty girls of the town, a fight breaks out. Milly doesn't know what more to do to tame the Pontipees. Adam thinks he does: he drives his brothers into town, through a treacherous mountain pass, and encourages them to abduct the local girls who caught their eye. On the way home, they make enough noise to cause an avalanche, which closes the pass until spring arrives. The only thing Adam forgot was to bring a preacher to marry the six couples.

Many people had a hand in making this delightful film as good as it could be. The screenplay is credited to the husband-and-wife team of Albert Hackett and Frances Goodrich, but they reportedly didn't get along with director Donen, who sent for another "old hand," Dorothy Kingsley. Young viewers who misread the script's intentions should remember that it was crafted by two forward-thinking women screenwriters. When Adam sings

"Bless Your Beautiful Hide" at the beginning of the movie, it's to illustrate how little he thinks of women—one's as good as another, more or less. Over the course of the film, he learns that love is the ingredient that can transform a servant girl into a life partner and a blowhard like himself into a caring husband and father. The ultimate lesson: people can change if they really want to.

The film was made at a time when the musical—or to put a finer point on it, the MGM musical—was becoming an endangered species. The lackluster box-office returns on some recent releases, like *The Band Wagon* (1953) and aquatic star vehicles for Esther Williams, caused studio chief Dore Schary to put the brakes on spending in this expensive genre. Both Gene Kelly and director Vincente Minnelli were disheartened to learn that the studio wouldn't give them the money to make *Brigadoon* (1954) on location in Scotland, as they had planned. Corners were also cut on *Seven Brides*, which was shot almost entirely on sets and soundstages at the Culver City MGM lot, with painted backdrops (some more obvious than others) having to substitute for the wide open spaces of Oregon.

Every time I've seen this movie with an audience, the "Lonesome Polecat" lyrics produce big laughs. "A man can't sleep / when he sleeps with sheep" is matched by "can't make no vows / to a herd of cows." Mercer biographer Gene Lees is dismissive of the songs in this film, but we beg to differ. Rhyming "twittering" and "baby sittering" in "Spring, Spring, Spring" is a clever turn of phrase. Mercer and DePaul teamed up again to write the score for another lively musical that made the transition from Broadway to Hollywood: *Li'l Abner* (1959), which was also choreographed on stage by Michael Kidd. His integration of ballet into the synchronized movements of the brothers chopping wood is just one indication of his inventiveness.

Sidebar: Many years ago, while hosting a tribute to *Mary Poppins* (1964) at the Academy of Motion Picture Arts and Sciences, I was chatting with Dee Dee Wood, who choreographed the Disney film with her then-husband Marc Breaux. It suddenly occurred to me that there was a similarity between the chimney sweep routine in *Poppins* and the vibrant dancing in *Li'l Abner*. Dee Dee instantly replied, "Of course. We were Michael Kidd's assistants, and we stole everything we could from him." So there is a natural through line from *Seven Brides for Seven Brothers* to *Mary Poppins*.

In addition to his agility, Russ Tamblyn was a good actor—and one of my (Jessie's) first crushes. He gives an endearing performance as Gideon, the youngest of the family, who all bear biblical names: Adam, Benjamin, Caleb, Daniel, Ephraim, and Frankincense (Frank for short). Tommy Rall is a truly gifted dancer whose charisma comes through in every scene he's in; you can see him arm-wrestling one of the townsmen in the big barn-raising number. Rall was a great talent who arrived in Hollywood just as the movie musical was dying out. But he's worth watching in such 1950s films as *Kiss Me Kate* (1953) and *My Sister Eileen* (1955). If you'll allow me (Leonard) to name-drop, Gene Kelly told me that he thought Tommy Rall was the most talented all-around performer of his time.

Five of seven brides and brothers

That's not to slight the contributions of Marc Platt, Matt Mattox, or Jacques d'Amboise of the New York City Ballet. These superb dancers all get a chance to shine, but the director was careful not to give d'Amboise very much to say because his New York accent was unmistakable.

As it turns out, MGM bet on the wrong horse that year. *Seven Brides for Seven Brothers* was a smash hit and enjoyed a long run in theaters, unlike *Brigadoon*. It was nominated for four Academy Awards and won for Best Scoring of a Musical, which went to Adolph Deutsch and Saul Chaplin.

It's difficult to describe the feelings that *Seven Brides for Seven Brothers* elicits in an audience—whether it's a theater full of fans or just you and your family at home. Jessie couldn't sit still as she played it over and over again. That was a long time ago, and we can't wait for her daughter to be old enough to appreciate the barn-raising number. We feel pretty sure she'll like it as much as her parents and grandparents do.

Milly's Stick-to-Your-Ribs Stew

This stew, much like Milly, can stand on its own two feet. The key here is time: low and slow. Feel free to cut the vegetables larger or smaller based on your preference. You can use a Dutch oven or a regular pot.

MAKES 4 SERVINGS

1 tablespoon garlic powder

Kosher salt and freshly ground black pepper

¼ cup all-purpose flour, divided

2 pounds stewing beef (such as sirloin, chuck, or round), cubed

½ cup olive oil

10 pearl onions

½ cup red wine

2 cups beef broth

1 garlic clove, minced

6 baby potatoes, quartered

3 large carrots, chopped

2 large celery ribs, chopped

2 sprigs fresh rosemary

2 teaspoons fresh thyme

2 teaspoons fresh parsley

1 tablespoon tomato paste

4 tablespoons (½ stick) butter, at room temperature

In a large bowl, combine the garlic powder, salt, pepper, and 2 tablespoons of flour. Add the beef to the bowl and toss to coat.

Heat the olive oil in large pot over medium-high heat. Add the beef and onions, sautéing until meat is browned.

Add the red wine, beef broth, and garlic, and stir to combine. Then stir in your potatoes, carrots, celery, rosemary, thyme, parsley, and tomato paste.

Thanks to this book, I have learned about the magic of beurre manié! It means "kneaded butter" in French and adds a bit of thickness to your stew. In a small bowl, mix the remaining flour and the butter together with your hands, until you form a paste. Add that paste to your stew and bring it to a boil. This will cook out the flour taste and release the starch.

Bring the heat down to a simmer. Cover and cook for 60 to 90 minutes, stirring occasionally. The beef should be extremely tender. Serve hot and enjoy!

Mary Badham and Gregory Peck as father and daughter in *To Kill a Mockingbird*

TO KILL A MOCKINGBIRD

(1962)

129 MINUTES

Directed by Robert Mulligan | **Produced by** Alan J. Pakula
Screenplay by Horton Foote; based on the novel by Harper Lee
Production design by Henry Bumstead | **Cinematography by** Russell Harlan
Music by Elmer Bernstein | **Cast:** Gregory Peck, Mary Badham, Philip Alford, Robert Duvall, John Megna, Frank Overton, Rosemary Murphy, Ruth White, Brock Peters, Estelle Evans, Paul Fix, Collin Wilcox, James Anderson

To many Americans, Atticus Finch is a hero; his superpower is his integrity, even in the face of injustice. Harper Lee set her debut novel in her Alabama hometown, Monroeville, renaming it Maycomb, and patterned its adult protagonist after her father, a small-town lawyer. In recent years much has been written about the very private author and her friendship with a local boy who turned out to be Truman Capote. He is depicted in the book as Dill Harris. She enjoyed all the attention she received as a Pulitzer Prize–winning author before he did, and it was a bone of contention between them.

Gregory Peck knew a good part when he saw it and became a coproducer of the film as well as its star. Atticus is an ennobling part, and it rubbed off on the popular star, who not only won an Academy Award for his performance but named it his all-time favorite role.

The setting is a small Southern town where everybody knows everybody as well as everybody else's business. The accusation of rape against Black workman Tom Robinson by a spoiled and coddled Mayella Violet Ewell is suspicious on the face of it. Atticus does his best to

Gregory Peck and Brock Peters in court

show the all-white jury that Mayella lured him into her home and instigated the incident—if it occurred. Before the trial is finished, a mob starts to gather one night, but Atticus talks them down by verbally recognizing friends and neighbors in the crowd and shaming them into breaking up and heading to their homes. But the jury is still out.

A major component of the film, like the book, is seeing Atticus through the eyes of his six-year-old daughter Scout and her ten-year-old brother Jem. They idolize their daddy and gain a new respect for him through the way he handles himself in court—and during the tense evening when a mob begins to assemble.

Producer (and not yet director) Alan J. Pakula competed to acquire the movie rights to Lee's best-selling book, which went on to sell millions of copies. He thought he would film it on location, but Maycomb didn't look the way it had in the 1930s, so it was carefully recreated on the Universal Pictures backlot by supervising art director Alexander Golitzen and his brilliant lieutenant, Henry Bumstead.

The film opens with a delicate and evocative title sequence, designed by Stephen Frankfurt, set to a perfect accompaniment by composer Elmer Bernstein. It is indicative of the care taken with this production at every turn. That extends to the casting as well. Mary Badham (whose

A very young Robert Duvall with an even younger Mary Badham in *To Kill a Mockingbird*

brother John went on to become a successful director) and Philip Alford are just right as the wide-eyed children who don't quite understand the tension that accompanies their father's latest court case—but do allow themselves to be spooked by the shadowy presence of a neighbor named Boo Radley. He remains unseen for most of the picture, but when he shows himself, he is played by Robert Duvall, in his first feature-film appearance.

The story shows its age in certain ways and definitely represents a white person's point of view, but no one has ever quarreled with its depiction of the Jim Crow South. The film won Oscars for Peck, screenwriter Foote, composer Bernstein, and art directors Golitzen and Bumstead. It was also Oscar-nominated as Best Picture. It has enjoyed a long life as required viewing in many school curricula, and to their credit, Mary Badham and Philip Alford have visited many classrooms over the years.

Most recently, *To Kill a Mockingbird* made its debut as a Broadway play, rewritten by Aaron Sorkin, who freshened the material and dared to be critical of Atticus Finch. That led to a lawsuit from Harper Lee's estate and a countersuit by Sorkin—both of which were settled, without details being revealed. But that doesn't negate the movie by any means.

Harper Lee's Crackling Cornbread

Harper Lee was known for making this Crackling Cornbread and now we're going to give it a shot. What is crackling, you ask? It's the rendered fat from a pig, obviously.

MAKES 6-8 CORNBREAD SLICES

5 strips bacon

3 tablespoons all-purpose flour

1½ cups white cornmeal

1 teaspoon kosher salt

1 teaspoon baking powder

1 large egg

1 cup milk

Cracklings (the residue from frying pig fat)

Preheat the oven to 450°F. In a medium skillet, cook the bacon until crispy. Transfer the bacon to a plate and set aside (you can eat it with your cornbread). Pour the bacon grease into a glass.

In a large bowl, combine the flour, cornmeal, salt, baking powder, egg, and milk. Carefully stir in about half of the bacon grease.

Grease a heavy ovenproof 9-inch skillet or a muffin tin with the other half of the bacon grease. Pour your batter into the pan of your choice. Bake for about 15 minutes, or until brown. Let cool and serve.

Mary Poppins gets better acquainted with her young charges, Jane and Michael Banks.

MARY POPPINS

(1964)

139 MINUTES

Presented by Walt Disney | **Directed by** Robert Stevenson
Produced by Bill Walsh | **Animation director:** Hamilton Luske
Screenplay by Bill Walsh and Don Da Gradi; based on the books by P. L. Travers
Design consultant: Tony Walton | **Cinematography by** Edward Colman
Musical direction by Irwin Kostal | **Songs by** Richard M. Sherman and Robert B. Sherman | **Special processes by** Ub Iwerks | **Visual effects by** Peter Ellenshaw, Eustace Lycett, and Robert A. Mattey | **Cast:** Julie Andrews, Dick Van Dyke, David Tomlinson, Glynis Johns, Hermione Baddeley, Reta Shaw, Karen Dotrice, Matthew Garber, Ed Wynn, Jane Darwell, Arthur Malet, Elsa Lanchester, Arthur Treacher, Reginald Owen, Don Barclay, Marjorie Bennett

Walt Disney had a list of accomplishments a mile long, but in the world of moviemaking, *Mary Poppins* was his masterpiece: the culmination of everything he had learned about entertainment since the 1920s. The project grew in importance with each new step and became the most expensive (and lucrative) film he ever made . . . also the best.

Walt's daughters Diane and Sharon first read one of P. L. Travers's books in the 1940s and brought it to their father's attention. He made inquiries about the screen rights and was rebuffed . . . but the character of the practically perfect English nanny stayed in his mind for years to follow. Finally, in the early 1960s, he paid a visit to the British author himself. Walt's list of achievements was of little concern to her, and he left without a deal. He then invited her to come to California and meet some of her potential collaborators, but he wisely flew the coop for the week she spent in Burbank. Songwriters Richard and Robert Sherman tape-recorded their

Four penguin waiters are falling over themselves to take care of their special guests, Mary and Bert, in the extended "Jolly Holiday" sequence.

meetings with the irritable and impossible author. That a film, let alone a great one, emerged from this series of stalemate meetings is little short of a miracle. (It was very well dramatized in the 2016 feature film *Saving Mr. Banks*, with Tom Hanks as Disney and Emma Thompson as Mrs. Travers).

The Poppins books didn't tell stories; instead, they offered sequences of life in the Banks household after the resourceful nanny comes into their home. Walt had circled his favorite chapters in a copy of the book. He gave another copy to the Sherman Brothers to read, and, as luck would have it, they circled the very same chapters. That's another reason the film works so well: the songs were directly inspired by the content of the books and were conceived in concert with Don Da Gradi's story outline (as seen in a series of pencil drawings).

The Sherman brothers were by now full-time employees who reported directly to Walt, who enjoyed having his in-house songwriters available for any and all assignments: a title tune for a segment of the Disneyland TV show, a catchy song for a Disneyland attraction, or in this case, a full-blown song score for a feature film to be sung mostly by Julie Andrews (who had a four-octave range).

Inspiration for *Mary Poppins* songs came from unexpected sources. The very British matte artist at the studio, Peter Ellenshaw, recalled the jaunty "Knees Up, Mother Brown" tune he heard as a young man observing buskers in the streets of London. The Shermans took the rhythmic spine of the song and paraphrased it as "Step in Time." Robert's son told his father about being inoculated for polio at school and swallowing a sugar cube to dispel the bitter taste of the vaccine. That led to "A Spoonful of Sugar" (". . . helps the medicine go down").

When Walt and his wife Lillian visited New York City, they got tickets to see Lerner and Loewe's Broadway musical *Camelot* and were enchanted by its leading lady, Julie Andrews. They went backstage to meet her, and Walt essentially offered her a job on the spot. This wasn't just any future boss: it was Walt Disney! He subsequently rented a house for her near his studio, waited out her pregnancy, and hired her husband Tony Walton to design the sets and the costumes.

Because it is designed to be episodic, the movie breaks down into a number of

Bert (Dick Van Dyke) leads his fellow chimney sweeps in a high-energy rooftop dance that had its roots in Michael Kidd's approach to *Seven Brides for Seven Brothers*.

What's a little chimney soot among friends?

loosely connected chapters, beginning with the firing of the Banks family's previous nanny (Elsa Lanchester) and Jane and Michael's singing want ad specifying what they desire in her replacement. Their father has no patience with this. He doesn't believe in coddling his children. But when all the other applicants literally blow away from his doorstep, that clears a path for the arrival of Mary Poppins.

Everything that happens from here onward is enacted with a touch of magic. What makes this even more effective is that the source of this unreality is never discussed. When Mary slides upstairs on the banister, or removes large items from her seemingly bottomless carpetbag, it's just the way she functions. A carved parrot on her parasol talks to her. What are you going to do about it? Her friend Bert the chimney sweep draws sidewalk images with colored chalk; with a snap of the fingers all four of them (Jane, Michael, Mary, and Bert) shrink in size and enter the colorful world of the drawing where they enjoy a "Jolly Holiday" with Mary.

After joining Walt for lunch at the studio one day, where he was wooing British star Glynis Johns to play Mrs. Banks, he mentioned the wonderful song "the boys" had written for her. That was patently untrue—and the Shermans' cue to make a beeline for their piano and create one. They repurposed a song they'd been writing for an entirely different character, and no one was any the wiser. "Sister Suffragette" gives Johns a great showcase that helps define her character and the period in which the film takes place.

As Mr. Banks explains, King Edward is on the throne, and it's "the age of men." Actor David Tomlinson utilizes the same *sprechgesang* approach—reciting the words rather than singing them—that Rex Harrison perfected in *My Fair Lady* (1964), enabling him to perform the Shermans' custom-tailored songs with zest.

The environment in which the film takes place is so appealing that it might not occur to a casual viewer that it was shot entirely on a soundstage at the Disney studio. Matte artist Peter Ellenshaw painted 102 glass images to indicate an aerial view of London and its rooftops.

Each supporting role is filled by a veteran character actor, from Reginald Owen as Admiral Boom to Arthur Treacher as the neighborhood police officer. I became familiar with some of these performers from seeing them in almost every Disney film, even after Walt's passing. Jane Darwell, the unforgettable Ma Joad in John Ford's *The Grapes of Wrath* (1940) was Disney's personal choice to play the Bird Lady. Ed Wynn, who plays Uncle Albert, was one of Walt's longtime favorites. His first gig for the studio was voicing the Mad Hatter in the animated *Alice in Wonderland* (1951), and he turned up in many Disney films of the 1960s. (You might say his presence is still felt today; actor Alan Tudyk as King Candy does a wonderful impression of Wynn on the soundtrack of 2012's *Wreck-It Ralph* and other recent Disney releases.)

Mary Poppins is a film for the ages, but even so, someone decided to create a sequel in 2018. Fortunately, all the people who worked on *Mary Poppins Returns* were fans of the original, including screenwriter David Magee (whose other credits include 2004's *Finding Neverland*), producer-director and cowriter Rob Marshall, composer Marc Shaiman, and most of the principal actors. I think of *Mary Poppins Returns* as a footnote to Walt Disney's career, and an agreeable one, but it clearly rides on the coattails of the 1964 masterpiece. Incidentally, two of the original stars (Dick Van Dyke and Karen Dotrice) make cameo appearances in the sequel.

Pineapple Upside-Down Cake

Mary Poppins deserves something silly and delicious. Have fun creating this somewhat ridiculous dessert—and if the topping gets stuck to the cake pan after flipping, scoop that right on out. It's still practically perfect. It's the kind of treat Uncle Albert might serve at a tea party.

MAKES 1 9-INCH CAKE

FOR THE TOPPING:

1 cup brown sugar

½ cup (1 stick) unsalted butter

1 can pineapple slices

FOR THE CAKE:

Nonstick cooking spray or butter

1 cup (2 sticks) unsalted butter, at room temperature

1½ granulated sugar

4 large eggs

¾ teaspoon vanilla extract

1½ cups all-purpose flour

5 tablespoons cake flour

5 tablespoons almond meal

¾ teaspoon baking powder

½ teaspoon kosher salt

¾ cup full-fat plain Greek yogurt

Maraschino cherries

Preheat the oven to 325°F and grease a 9-inch cake pan with nonstick cooking spray or butter.

Prepare the topping. In a small saucepan, heat the brown sugar and butter over medium heat, without stirring, until the sugar dissolves and the mixture is bubbling, about 5 minutes. Pour your caramel mixture into the greased pan. Arrange the pineapple rings on top of the caramel. Set aside.

Prepare the cake batter. In a medium bowl, combine the butter and sugar using an electric mixer. Add in one egg at a time, beating in between. Beat in the vanilla extract.

In a separate medium bowl, combine the flours, almond meal, baking powder, and salt. Slowly add this mixture to your wet ingredients and stir gently to combine. Stir in the Greek yogurt.

Pour the batter into the pan and bake for 1 hour. Remove from the oven and wait 5 minutes before flipping it over onto a plate. Place cherries on top.

Maria distracts the von Trapp children by singing about her favorite things.

THE SOUND OF MUSIC

(1965)

152 MINUTES

Produced and directed by Robert Wise
Screenplay by Ernest Lehman; based on the Broadway play by Howard Lindsay and Russell Crouse, which is based on the book by Maria von Trapp
Music supervisor: Irwin Kostal | **Choreography by** Marc Breaux and Dee Dee Wood
Photography by Ted McCord | **Songs by** Richard Rodgers and Oscar Hammerstein II
New songs by Richard Rodgers | **Cast:** Julie Andrews, Christopher Plummer, Eleanor Parker, Richard Haydn, Peggy Wood, Charmian Carr, Heather Menzies, Nicholas Hammond, Duane Chase, Angela Cartwright, Debbie Turner, Kym Karath, Anna Leel, Ben Wright, Norma Varden

The Sound of Music is one of the best-loved movies of all time. It was the biggest box-office success of 1965, and then the biggest moneymaking movie of all time—a record it maintained for five years. People of all ages, everywhere, took this film to their hearts in a way no other could replace. One cinema in Europe showed it continuously for three solid years!

Why?

First, it was Julie Andrews's follow-up to her smashing screen debut in *Mary Poppins*. People couldn't get enough of her. And she was singing the glorious Rodgers and Hammerstein songs that had made *The Sound of Music* a smash on Broadway, where it ran for nearly four years.

Next, it is about a family, a real-life family, making it widely relatable. It is filled with singable Rodgers and Hammerstein songs, from an era when songs from Broadway shows became hit records and slid into the zeitgeist. "Do Re Mi," "My Favorite Things," "Edelweiss," and "Climb Ev'ry Mountain" are part of the fabric that is twentieth-century American music.

What a wonderful way to show off Salzburg.

Director-producer Robert Wise, who made the Oscar-winning *West Side Story*, again assembled a team that would draw out the best of the already-proven ingredients. They strengthened the book of the show, jettisoned several songs that nobody missed, and completely rewrote the script. That was the work of screenwriter Ernest Lehman, who had already done right by Rodgers and Hammerstein for the film version of *The King and I* (1956). Associate producer Saul Chaplin, a veteran songwriter himself, had a hand in shaping the score.

The filmmakers also urged Richard Rodgers to add two new songs to the score, providing both music and lyrics, as his longtime writing partner Oscar Hammerstein II had died in 1960. Rodgers accepted the challenge and contributed two new numbers that help us understand the character makeup of Maria: "I Have Confidence" expresses her nervousness on the morning she shows up at the von Trapp residence, and "Something Good" tells us that she doesn't take her relationship with the Captain for granted.

The story has more spine, and relevance, than it did on stage. A card in the opening titles tells us that the setting is Salzburg, Austria, "in the last golden days of the 1930s." There is just a taste of fore-

A unique feature of the Broadway play and film is the "Lonely Goatherd" number devised by the premier puppeteers of their generation, Bil and Cora Baird. We're not sure even the gifted von Trapp children could have successfully manipulated those marionettes!

shadowing in the first half of the film; it is the second half, approaching a climax, when the threat of Nazi takeover comes to the fore. This threatening undercurrent is in sharp contrast to the movie's goody-goody reputation.

The surest sign that we're in the hands of a master filmmaker is how the movie opens. Everyone who has ever seen it knows that Julie Andrews is singing to herself while whirling around on a grassy mountaintop in the Alps. But watch the film again from the beginning (a very good place to start), and you'll see that her glorious burst of song comes after three full minutes of silent aerial footage showing the majesty and mystery of the cloudy, snowy mountain range. Then we hear flutes, which give way to a full orchestra as Andrews, overcome with feelings for her surroundings, sings "The hills are alive / with the sound of music . . ."

Wise's experience as a film editor—apprenticing on some of the Fred Astaire–Ginger Rogers musicals of the 1930s and editing *Citizen Kane* (1941) at RKO Radio Pictures—came in handy when it was decided to perform one of the show's

Maria (Julie Andrews) and Captain von Trapp (Christopher Plummer) join the children for a final concert before they flee for the border.

most popular songs, "Do Re Mi," in a constantly moving cavalcade of Maria and the children at some of Salzburg's most beautiful locations. The staging and editing of this number make it a visual and musical highlight. Veteran cinematographer Ted McCord, whose career dated back to the silent-film era, made virtually every shot in the film a beauty. One can admire the artful composition of every widescreen shot, without it ever calling attention to itself.

In order to accept and enjoy this entertaining movie, one must put "fidelity to the truth" on hold. The real Captain von Trapp and the real Maria bear no resemblance to the people depicted here. The family did escape from the Nazis with little time to spare, but they stepped onto a train platform rather than scaling a series of mountains to gain freedom. Maria von Trapp told her story for the first time in a 1949 book, on which the stage musical was officially based.

Given that this was only her third movie, Julie Andrews had the good fortune to work with the same musical director (Irwin Kostal) and choreographers (Marc Breaux and Dee Dee Wood) she had teamed up with for *Mary Poppins*. Director Robert Wise wanted his newly minted star to be seen and heard at her best.

If we regard the now-famous title song sequence as a prologue, the film officially begins inside the abbey where Maria is a novitiate. Nonnberg Abbey is presided over by Mother Abbess (Peggy Wood), who sums up her feelings in song: "How Do You Solve a Problem Like Maria?" Telling the enthusiastic and sincere young woman that life as a nun is not meant for her, she sends her out in the world to fill a job: governess to the seven children belonging to widower Captain von Trapp, who lives in a villa outside of town. She immediately understands that the children feel constrained by their father's unforgiving rules and, in the course of time, persuades him to spend more time getting to know his offspring. The magic key is music. Today, one might call it the family's love language.

If the storytelling in *The Sound of Music* seems unhurried, especially in the second half, that's because it was intended as a "road-show" attraction: in the first few months of its release in the US it was shown just twice a day, matinee and evening performances—like a Broadway play. If you own or rent the Blu-ray Disc, it includes the original "Intermission" card and the instrumental music that played as an entr'acte.

Christopher Plummer hits just the right dramatic notes as the Captain, hard and inflexible at first but believably warm and loving as the pieces of his life fall into proper place. The actor famously belittled *The Sound of Music* before, during, and after its production but ultimately made his peace with it, even costarring with Julie Andrews in a television version of *On Golden Pond*.

Beautiful Eleanor Parker is perfectly cast as the wealthy Baroness who hopes to ensnare Captain von Trapp as her husband—more for show than any other reason. Humorist Richard Haydn fulfills the screenplay's need for a friend that the main characters can talk to, but fans of his work may regret that he doesn't have more to do than serve that function. And British character actor Ben Wright is suitably menacing, without resorting to elaborate histrionics, as the town official who represents the Nazi party. (The only other Nazi we encounter up close is Rolf, the telegram messenger who falls in love with Liesl, the eldest of the von Trapp children, and sings "You Are Sixteen, Going on Seventeen.")

The Sound of Music has inspired revivals of the show, sing-along presentations, and ongoing tours of Salzburg that reveal to visitors from around the globe the sights they have glimpsed in the movie. That there is still demand for this tour says more than anything else possibly could about a sixty-year-old film.

One of Maria's Favorite Things...

Doorbells and sleigh bells are fine in their place, but we prefer to offer you a traditional Austrian entrée that may well become one of your favorite things, chicken schnitzel. To make cooking the chicken easier, you can slice each breast into thirds.

MAKES 4 SERVINGS

2 eggs

Juice of 1 lemon, plus additional, for garnish

½ cup chicken broth

¼ cup white wine

2 cups breadcrumbs

1 cup all-purpose flour

1 cup grated Parmesan cheese

1 teaspoon salted butter

2 garlic cloves, minced

1 teaspoon dried parsley, plus additional, for garnish

1 teaspoon onion powder

1 teaspoon garlic powder

3 tablespoons kosher salt, divided

Freshly ground black pepper

1½–2 pounds boneless skinless chicken breasts

2 tablespoons olive oil

1 package egg noodles

Make the schnitzel first. In a medium bowl, combine the eggs, lemon juice, chicken broth, and wine. In a separate medium bowl, combine the breadcrumbs, flour, cheese, butter, garlic, parsley, onion powder, garlic powder, salt, and pepper.

Brine the chicken in a bowl of cold water with 2 tablespoons of salt for 15 minutes, then transfer the chicken to a cutting board. Using a meat mallet/tenderizer, pound the chicken breasts to an even thickness.

Submerge a chicken breast in the egg mixture, then evenly coat it with your flour mixture. Repeat for all breasts.

In a large nonstick skillet, heat the oil over medium heat until shimmering. Place two chicken breasts in the pan and cook until the first side is golden brown, 2 to 3 minutes. Flip and cook for another 2 to 3 minutes, then transfer to a plate. Repeat with the remaining breasts.

Cook the noodles according to package instructions. Serve immediately with your crispy chicken schnitzel. You can top with more parsley and lemon juice, if desired.

This movie's not-so-secret weapon: Gene Wilder

WILLY WONKA AND THE CHOCOLATE FACTORY

(1971)

100 MINUTES

Directed by Mel Stuart | **Produced by** David L. Wolper and Stan Margulies
Screenplay by Roald Dahl | **Cinematography by** Arthur Ibbetson
Musical direction by Walter Scharf | **Songs by** Anthony Newley and Leslie Bricusse
Art direction by Harper Goff | **Cast:** Gene Wilder, Jack Albertson, Peter Ostrum, Roy Kinnear, Julie Dawn Cole, Leonard Stone, Denise Nickerson, Nora Denney, Paris Themmen, Ursula Reit, Michael Bollner, Diana Sowle, Günter Meisner

Roald Dahl was a successful writer whose stories formed the basis for a number of movies, including *The Witches* (1990), *James and the Giant Peach* (1996), *Matilda* (1996), and *The BFG* (2016). While several of those adaptations did justice to their source material, none has enjoyed the affection and enduring popularity of *Willy Wonka and the Chocolate Factory*, which began life as a novel called *Charlie and the Chocolate Factory*. Dahl wrote the screenplay himself, although it was revised by David Seltzer with input from director Mel Stuart.

Charlie Bucket is a poor boy who delivers newspapers to help his family pay the rent. Every day he passes by Willy Wonka's Chocolate Factory, which had been shuttered for several years. Then, the reclusive owner declares that he is circulating five Wonka Bars with Golden Tickets that will entitle the buyers to visit the factory and earn a lifetime supply of chocolate. There are some detours along the way, but Charlie emerges as a winner and takes his grandpa Joe along. As the promised tour begins the children are forced to sign detailed contracts, and one by

Violet Beauregarde meets an appropriate—but unseemly—end.

one they are dispatched because of their greedy ways, along with their parents. Charlie is the last one remaining, but Willy Wonka is an unpredictable fellow and there is no guarantee he will make good on his promise.

It may come as a surprise to learn that the film was not a box-office hit when it was first released in 1971. It took repeated showings on television and a long life on home video to build a worldwide following, and it is now part of the zeitgeist. One still finds references to it in contemporary movies and TV shows. Admittedly, some of that is due to the fact that it was remade twice, both times featuring popular stars—Johnny Depp in the 2005 version directed by Tim Burton, which reverted to the name *Charlie and the Chocolate Factory*, and Timothée Chalamet in 2023's *Wonka*.

But those films, which boast of cutting-edge visual effects that the creators of the 1971 musical could only dream of, are missing one indelible ingredient that cannot be duplicated: Gene Wilder.

In his book *Pure Imagination*, director Stuart remembers the moment that Wilder, not yet a household name, walked into their production office to audition for the role. He turned to producer David L. Wolper and said excitedly, "He's our Willy Wonka." He was so certain of it that he chased the actor down the hallway to the elevator bank and told him as much.

As talented as Johnny Depp and Timothée Chalamet are, they lack the inscrutability of Wilder's Wonka. Is he sincere or a trickster? He can be cold as ice one moment and lovable the next, as he spouts quotations from sources as varied as William Shakespeare and Oscar Wilde. He is completely unpredictable.

Because the character of Willy Wonka is so opaque, it was vital to cast warm-hearted actors in the other principal roles: the unknown Peter Ostrum as Charlie Bucket and show-business veteran Jack Albertson as his Grandpa Joe. Ostrum was found in a nationwide search led by legendary casting director Marion Dougherty. As part of a Cleveland, Ohio, theater troupe he was already a professional actor at the age of twelve. He is charismatic without ever seeming "cute," the kind of everyday kid you want to root for. His character is also an underdog who lives with his mother and four bedridden grandparents (a typical Roald Dahl touch) without complaint.

Albertson was a veteran of Broadway and Hollywood with a Tony Award and an Oscar to his credit, for the stage and screen versions of *The Subject Was Roses* (1968). He later reached his biggest audience as costar of the TV comedy series *Chico and the Man* and added an Emmy to his award shelf in the process. Like Ostrum, he exudes a natural warmth and likability.

Another crucial factor in the enduring appeal of the film is its song score by Anthony Newley and Leslie Bricusse. Already established for their stage musicals *Stop the World–I Want to Get Off* and *The Roar of the Greasepaint–the Smell of the Crowd* (both of which starred Newley in their original London productions as well as on Broadway), they were responsible for such hit songs as "What Kind of Fool Am I?" which won a Grammy Award as Song of the Year in

Jack Albertson as Grandpa Joe and Peter Ostrum as Charlie Bucket

1961, "Feeling Good," and the title song for the James Bond movie *Goldfinger* (1964). For *Willy Wonka*, they provided several memorable numbers, including "The Candy Man," "Pure Imagination," and "I've Got a Golden Ticket," and at least one dud, "Cheer Up, Charlie."

If the name Mel Stuart doesn't ring a bell, that's because he spent the majority of his career working in the documentary field, initially for esteemed television producer David L. Wolper (his boss and then partner for seventeen years). He later branched out into other types of films, including mainstream commercial movies like *If This Is Tuesday It Must Be Belgium* (1969) and *One Is a Lonely Number* (1972). He also served as a producer of scores of TV movies, miniseries, and "event" documentaries like *The Making of the President* (1960), *Four Days in November* (1964), and *Wattstax* (1973).

He wound up with an Emmy, a Peabody Award, and an Academy Award nomination for this film.

Both he and producer Wolper were venturing into unknown territory in tackling a musical fantasy, but they were wise enough to surround themselves with talented people who could fully realize the potential in Roald Dahl's inventive story. By shooting in and around Munich, Germany, they gave their film an otherworldly fairy-tale quality worthy of the Brothers Grimm. Ask your family if they recognize where the story takes place—and when—and see how they respond. Art direction was placed in the experienced hands of Harper Goff, who designed Walt Disney's *20,000 Leagues Under the Sea* (1954).

Elements that might date the movie become part of its charm. A character like Mike Teevee wouldn't be dressed like a cowboy in today's world, but his obsession with television is still easily relatable. The same goes for his fellow contestants. Who hasn't encountered a greedy little kid like Veruca Salt at one point in their life? Or a glutton like Augustus Gloop?

As to the Oompa-Loompas, they are as vital to the movie as any of the leading players. It was necessity, not inspiration, that caused Stuart to paint their faces and bodies orange, as Dahl's description of them—illustrated in the first printings of his book—were politically incorrect, to put it mildly.

Willy Wonka and the Chocolate Factory ranks alongside *The Wizard of Oz* as one of the all-time great musical fantasies. It is proof positive that good ideas, expertly executed, make for movies that defy the passage of time.

Splendiferously Indulgent Cupcakes

How could we possibly capture the wildly imaginative Wonka world in one dish? It's a nearly impossible task! The only real answer is candy. You need to walk down the candy aisle and pick up everything you love. And we mean everything. The more candy (and color), the better.

MAKES 6 LARGE CUPCAKES OR 12 MINIS

FOR THE CUPCAKES:

Nonstick cooking spray or butter

2 cups all-purpose flour

2½ teaspoons baking powder

¼ teaspoon kosher salt

4 large eggs

1½ cups granulated sugar

1 cup whole milk

1 tablespoon vanilla extract

1 tablesoon vegetable oil

FOR THE TOPPINGS:

1 tub frosting (your choice of flavor)

Candies of choice

Preheat the oven to 350°F and grease a muffin tin with nonstick cooking spray or butter, or insert cupcake liners.

Whisk the flour, baking powder, and salt in a medium bowl. Set aside.

Add the eggs to a large bowl, then use an electric mixer to slowly mix in your sugar. You want it to look like pale fluff (yes, that's a technical term).

Slowly start adding your flour mixture to the "pale fluff," using the electric mixer to gently combine. Add in your milk, vanilla, and oil, and combine again. The batter should be very smooth.

Pour the batter into your muffin tin, filling each well to just under the top. Bake for about 30 minutes, or until golden brown.

After removing the cupcakes from the oven, let them cool to room temperature. Now comes the fun part: frost your cupcakes and start decorating with the candies!

The sheriff and his deputies take Nathan Morgan away from his home and family in a tense moment from *Sounder.*

SOUNDER

(1972)

95 MINUTES

Produced by Robert B. Radnitz | **Directed by** Martin Ritt
Screenplay by Lonne Elder III; based on the novel by William H. Armstrong
Cinematography by John A. Alonso | **Music by** Taj Mahal | **Production design by** Walter Herndon | **Cast:** Cicely Tyson, Paul Winfield, Kevin Hooks, Carmen Mathews, Taj Mahal, James Best, Eric Hooks, Yvonne Jarrell, Sylvia "Kuumba" Williams, Janet MacLachlan

It would be nice if we could recommend many classic films that portray a variety of races, ethnicities, and nationalities in a positive light. But until the twenty-first century, few movies told stories that reflected life outside the white world. That makes the handful of exceptions stand out all the more: *Sounder* is an outstanding example.

The Morgan family are sharecroppers, working hard to earn a living in Louisiana during the Great Depression of the 1930s. Their only escape is the occasional baseball game and the pleasure they derive from music, as sung and played by a native troubadour (played by bluesman Taj Mahal). They toil over the land owned by the local grocer, taking their payment out in trade. The oldest son, David (Kevin Hooks), enjoys hunting with his father, Nathan (Paul Winfield), and their loyal hound dog Sounder, but one fateful night, the racoon they're chasing gets away, which means dinner will be sparse. The next morning, there is fresh ham on the breakfast table. When Rebecca (Cicely Tyson) asks her husband how it got there, he says, simply, "I did what I had to do." Later that day, the sheriff arrests Nathan (Paul Winfield) for stealing the ham. Sounder follows the wagon that carries Nathan away, and a deputy shoots the dog, who disappears

Cicely Tyson as Rebecca, the bedrock of the Morgan family. This performance earned her an Oscar nomination.

to lick his wounds. Eventually he returns home, but he is not the same and doesn't bark. Nathan receives a one-year sentence of hard labor, but the sheriff won't tell Rebecca where he is being held. A kind white woman intercedes and finds out the information. David makes the arduous journey to that prison camp. On his way home he happens upon a school for Black children where an enlightened teacher named Miss Camille (Janet McLachlan) piques his curiosity, showing him books about African American men of achievement, past and present. He yearns to become one of her students, but when his father returns home with an injured leg, he understands that he must stay and toil alongside his family. The boy is at a crossroads in his young life—but at least Sounder is home and back to his old self.

Unlike many other films portraying Black families positively, *Sounder* did not go unnoticed by critics or audiences in 1972. It was a financial success and earned four Academy Award nominations, including Best Picture and record-breaking honors for Cicely Tyson, Paul Winfield, and screenwriter Lonne Elder III.

And unlike other films of this period, it doesn't date at all—in part because it is so good, but also because it is already a period piece. Little explanation is required for your family to accept the

Morgans' trials and tribulations as part of everyday life in the South during the 1930s. The actions and reactions of the landowner and the sheriff are unpleasant (to put it mildly) but based on truth. Black people were downtrodden, and there were few remedies for their lot in life. But some families, like the one depicted here, make every effort to rise above their circumstances.

The key roles are played to perfection. Cicely Tyson brings rich humanity to her portrayal of Rebecca, who works herself to the bone and never complains. She doesn't so much play the character as *become* her; that was her stock in trade. Paul Winfield is also ideal as a proud man who fulfills his role as father and husband to the letter. Like Jean Valjean in *Les Miserables*, when his family is hungry, he puts food on the table, even if it means he has to steal it. Rebecca feels obliged to say something to the grocer who holds her family hostage about the unfairness of it all, but the minute he reacts, she moves on. She knows full well the price of speaking out. Even the nice woman who tries to coax the sheriff into telling her where Nathan is being held is reprimanded for stepping over the line. This is Louisiana in 1933. Wishing it were different wouldn't change anything.

Kevin Hooks and his canine costar, Sounder

Sounder never surrenders to melodrama. The dog is a perfect companion for the father and son when they go hunting . . . and he feels the pain of Nathan's forced departure as keenly as any of the other family members.

Sounder was written by William H. Armstrong and published in 1970 and won the Newberry Medal, the most esteemed prize given for young-adult literature. The film rights were acquired by producer Robert B. Radnitz, who took it to 20th Century Fox. Radnitz was known as a man who cared about quality entertainment for family audiences, and he translated many popular and widely

Taj Mahal's music is heard throughout the movie.

admired books for the screen, including *A Dog of Flanders* (1960), *Island of the Blue Dolphins* (1964), *My Side of the Mountain* (1969), *Where the Lilies Bloom* (1974), and *Cross Creek* (1983), which was nominated for four Oscars. His favorite director was Martin Ritt, who had a reputation for crafting good movies with forward-thinking social content like *Norma Rae* (1979, with Sally Field), *Hud* (1963), *Conrack* (1974), and *The Front* (1978), a potent story starring Woody Allen about the 1950s Communist witch hunt in the entertainment world. Ritt was a victim of blacklisting himself and seized the opportunity to dramatize what the experience was like. I (Leonard) once asked him how he regarded reviews, and he answered with a smile, "I'm never as bad as they say I am, and I'm never as great as they say I am."

A sequel, bearing the lumpy title *Part Two Sounder*, was released in 1976. Radnitz produced it from a screenplay by Lonne Elder III, but neither Ritt nor any of the leading actors returned from the 1972 original. (The lone exception was the participation of singer Taj Mahal.) It was not well received and is mostly forgotten.

However, in 2003, *The Wonderful World of Disney* commissioned a television remake of Armstrong's novel and, in a heartwarming move, hired Kevin Hooks, who played David in 1972, to direct it. He in turn called on Paul Winfield to costar in it, not as Nathan but as the schoolteacher who inspires David to learn about his heritage. This TV movie gets high marks for good intentions, but it can't compare to the original film.

Doggone-Good Gumbo

If we've learned anything about real Louisiana cooking, it's that everything begins with a good roux—and a heavy-bottomed pot. A roux is a mixture of equal parts flour and fat, sautéed over low to medium heat and used as a thickening agent for stews, soups, and sauces. The darker the roux, the richer the flavor.

MAKES 4 SERVINGS

⅔ cup (1⅓ stick) unsalted butter

1 cup all-purpose flour

12 ounces kielbasa or andouille sausage, sliced

6 cups chicken broth, divided

1 bunch celery, chopped

1 large yellow onion, chopped

1 large yellow bell pepper, chopped

3 garlic cloves, minced

1 bunch green onions, sliced

1 small jalapeño pepper, chopped

1 cup shredded rotisserie chicken

6–7 ounces precooked shrimp

Kosher salt, freshly ground black pepper, and Cajun seasoning

White rice, for serving

Let's make a roux! In a large heavy-bottomed pot, melt your butter over low heat. When it has liquified, add in the flour. Whisk together until there are no clumps. Keep stirring intermittently for about 45 minutes, or until you've achieved a chocolate-brown color.

While the roux is browning, add the sausage to a large skillet over medium-high heat. Cook for about 5 to 8 minutes, or until evenly browned, then transfer to a plate. Add ½ cup of chicken stock to the skillet to deglaze the pan, scraping the bottom to incorporate any browned bits. Pour the stock into your pot with the roux.

Add the celery, yellow onion, bell pepper, garlic, green onions, jalapeño, and the remaining 5½ cups of chicken stock to the pot and stir well. Bring to a boil over medium heat and cook for 5 minutes, or until the vegetables are tender. Skim off any foam that rises to the top of the pot.

Add the chicken, sausage, shrimp, and seasonings. Adjust to taste. Continue cooking on medium heat for another 5 minutes. Serve over white rice.

The interstellar dynamic duo: Han Solo and Chewbacca

STAR WARS

(1977)

121 MINUTES

Written and directed by George Lucas | **Produced by** Gary Kurtz
Cinematography by Gilbert Taylor | **Music by** John Williams | **Cast:** Mark Hamill, Harrison Ford, Carrie Fisher, Alec Guinness, Peter Cushing, Anthony Daniels, Kenny Baker, Peter Mayhew, David Prowse, Phil Brown, Shelagh Fraser, Jack Purvis

Never did I imagine that I (Leonard) would acquire street cred because of my interviews with George Lucas that appeared on the first VHS release of the *Star Wars* trilogy in 1995, which sold 25 million cassettes. I can't count the number of times I've been stopped by a young person who tells me that's where they first saw me—or, in some cases, fast-forwarded through my segment. It still happens all the time.

Star Wars is in a class of its own. Not just a financial success, it became a cultural phenomenon and remains so to this day. It has spawned sequels, spinoffs, ripoffs, artwork, and other fictional worlds in print and online. When the first film opened in 1977, some theater owners turned it down, as sci-fi films were generally considered B-movie fodder or kid stuff. It had no marquee value, either, as its stars (except Alec Guinness) were essentially unknowns.

What must it have felt like to pass on this movie? Ask the toymakers who didn't seize the opportunity to manufacture lightsabers and costumes. They missed out on Christmas sales that year; some even sold IOU receipts to eager customers. Most telling of all, in negotiations with 20th Century Fox, the studio gave George Lucas all rights to license and merchandise the film in perpetuity. That's how little it was valued before it opened.

R2-D2 , C-3PO, Obi-Wan Kenobi, and Luke Skywalker assess their options.

It was the fans who made *Star Wars* a hit—not the exhibitors, or the distributor, or the advertising people. Cash-paying customers who returned to see it again and again turned the tide. As we write this in 2025, the IP (intellectual property) is alive and well, with several spinoff series on Disney+ and more on the way.

In the course of time, Lucas retitled the film *Star Wars, Episode IV: A New Hope*, but when it opened in 1977, it was simply *Star Wars*. The on-screen text that opens the picture was a direct imitation of old-time Saturday matinee serials like *Flash Gordon* (1936), which began each episode with a recap of what had occurred in previous installments. Even the formatting of this introduction, with its paragraphs floating up the screen to a vanishing point, was an homage to *Flash Gordon*. But the story it tells is nothing like that 1930s comic strip by Alex Raymond.

This space saga starts simply enough on the planet Tatooine, as young Luke Skywalker begins another day of work on his uncle and aunt's farm, where he is reluctantly living. His friends have gone to The Academy, which is where he wants to be—but instead of setting off to find adventure, adventure finds him. A battle is growing for control of the Galactic Empire, and the intrepid Princess Leia is leading a resistance movement called the Rebel Alliance. She makes a hologram plea for help, installing it—and the blueprint of the Death Star—into the memory bank of R2-D2, a droid who ends up on Tatooine, along with his companion C-3PO. Luke joins them in their search for Obi-Wan Kenobi, the wise man who can advise them on how to defeat Darth Vader and save Princess Leia. Han Solo, a mercenary soldier of fortune, and Chewbacca, his gorilla-like Wookie sidekick, are hired to transport Luke and Obi-Wan to Alderaan on Han's ship, the Millennium Falcon. Along the way, Han Solo finds himself in the unlikely position of being a hero for once.

The *Star Wars* team created space battles that made the audience feel as if they were in the cockpits firing at their opponents. Here was the equivalent of a Western showdown, transposed to outer space, with speed and credibility beyond anything audiences had seen or experienced before.

Casting was crucial, as it required a commitment to a minimum of two sequels. It wouldn't be impossible to replace a prominent cast member midstream, so to speak, but it would be awkward, at best. It's difficult to imagine anyone else in these signature roles. That also holds true for Alec Guinness, the acclaimed, Oscar-winning British star who became familiar to at least two generations of moviegoers as Obi-Wan. As a director, Lucas had enormous respect for British actors, whose training and professionalism made his job easier. (Peter Cushing's death in 1994 seemed to spell the end of Grand Moff Tarkin's participation in these films, but with the approval of his estate, the veteran actor was digitally recreated for a small but significant part in 2016's *Rogue One: A Star Wars Story*.)

An active, not passive, heroine: Carrie Fisher as Princess Leia

It didn't take long for fans to learn who was hiding in plain sight: Anthony Daniels was C-3PO, Kenny Baker was R2-D2, Peter Mayhew was Chewbacca, and David Prowse wore the black helmet and costume of Darth Vader. The character's voice was easier to recognize as that of James Earl Jones, but he did not seek or receive screen credit.

The success of *Star Wars* depended heavily on visual effects, but no great strides had been made since Stanley Kubrick's *2001: A Space Odyssey* (1968) and the lesser-known *Silent Running* (1972). That's because science-fiction films were considered a slightly disreputable genre. So, Lucas had to build a team of experts and experimenters from

It's clear that Darth Vader means business.

scratch, led by John Dykstra, who worked on *Silent Running*. They became the core members of a new Lucas-owned company named Industrial Light & Magic. It set the gold standard for visual effects and became the spawning ground for a slew of competitors.

Since this origin story is now so familiar, it may seem simplistic and even hokey to kids who have ventured into new *Star Wars* realms depicted in TV series like *The Mandalorian*, which have built on the foundation that George Lucas created. But good origin stories are necessary and valuable, and none more so than this one.

Lucas grew up in the 1960s watching old movie serials, one chapter at a time, on local TV. (He replicated them in his next project, 1981's *Raiders of the Lost Ark*.) He also ingested a slew of low-budget science-fiction films. But when he got older, he immersed himself in the teachings of philosopher Joseph Campbell and took great interest in his foundational Hero's Journey structure. Applying the tenets of that storytelling template gave *Star Wars* additional weight and depth. You could say that Lucas's influences were both highbrow and lowbrow. That's one reason the films, especially the original trilogy, have enjoyed such approbation.

Your family is likely to see themselves in one of these archetypes. Is it Luke, the unintentional hero who "has greatness thrust upon him," as Shakespeare said? Is it Han Solo, the self-disparaging guy who sees himself as self-centered when in fact his heart is in the right place all along? Or is it Princess Leia, who's as brave as any man and keeps her eyes on the prize?

We can't emphasize enough the impact of the decision to make Leia an active, rather than passive, member of the heroic team in *Star Wars*. This was no damsel in distress. She served as a role model for girls and a hero to feminists and set a precedent for other filmmakers to follow.

The 1977 film also made overnight stars of its cast. Mark Hamill, Harrison Ford, and Carrie Fisher had all been paying their dues, working in movies and television but without much recognition. Suddenly, they were world-famous movie stars. Lucas responded to their work and talent by giving each of them a percentage of the film's profits, a rare gesture in the movie business.

Carrie Fisher grew up in a show-business family. Her father was popular singer Eddie Fisher, and her mother was the unsinkable Debbie Reynolds. One day Debbie came to the offices of *Entertainment Tonight* to shoot an interview with me (Leonard), and as she breezed through the entryway of our offices, she called out, "Goodbye, everyone . . . it's Princess Leia's mother . . . goodbye." The daughter's sudden and overpowering fame had eclipsed that of her movie-star mother's, and Debbie knew it, along with the whole wide world.

When I spoke to George Lucas in 1995 and asked him what one word would sum up the whole *Star Wars* experience for him, he replied, "Unpredictable . . . to this day. It's still an unfolding adventure."

"I started out in school as an anthropologist, and I was very interested in that sort of thing. Since college, I'd been interested in the fact that there was no modern fairy tale; there were no modern myths that our society created, other than the Western, which had been on the wane. So I said, gee, wouldn't it be great to do an outer space thing and create a modern mythology around a kind of space-opera-adventure, like *Flash Gordon* was."

Lucas faced rejection from several studios and then met with Alan Ladd Jr. at 20th Century Fox. "He said, 'I'm interested. I don't understand this, but I loved *American Graffiti*, and whatever you do is OK with me.' Otherwise, I don't think it would have ever gotten done, 'cause it was crazy: you know, spaceships and Wookies and robots. It was just unlike anything that had ever been seen before. It was hard for people to visualize it."

And now, all these years later, it continues to win new fans, as parents gleefully share it with their children. George Lucas put everything he had into creating this world, and it shows.

Lightsaber Skewers

You may not know this, but Storm Troopers are experts in the kitchen. Their precision chopping is a sight to behold. Charcoal can be hard to come by in space, so you can prepare these skewers on the stove.

MAKES 4 SERVINGS

2 tablespoons salted butter

1 pound boneless skinless chicken breasts, cubed

1 pound beef tenderloin tips

2 yellow bell peppers, cut into 1½-inch squares

2 orange bell peppers, cut into 1½-inch squares

2 red bell peppers, cut into 1½-inch squares

1 red onion, cut into 1½-inch squares

3 small red potatoes, quartered

10 large button mushrooms, halved

Kosher salt and freshly ground black pepper

Onion powder

Garlic powder

In a large skillet over medium heat, melt your butter. Add the chicken and tenderloin tips and sauté for about 10 minutes, stirring intermittently to evenly brown each side. Add all of the vegetables to the skillet, along with the salt, pepper, onion powder, and garlic powder. Stir to combine. Continue cooking, stirring intermittently, for about 5 to 8 minutes, or until the vegetables have begun to soften.

Remove from heat and let cool until cool enough to handle. Assemble your meat and vegetables on skewers (or lightsabers). Enjoy!

A close encounter of the first kind: E.T. examines Elliott for the first time.

E.T. THE EXTRA-TERRESTRIAL

(1982)

115 MINUTES

Produced by Steven Spielberg and Kathleen Kennedy
Directed by Steven Spielberg | **Screenplay by** Melissa Mathison
Cinematography by Allen Daviau | **Music by** John Williams
Cast: Henry Thomas, Drew Barrymore, Dee Wallace, Peter Coyote, Robert MacNaughton, C. Thomas Howell, Erika Eleniak

One of the most popular films of all time, *E.T. the Extra-Terrestrial* cemented Steven Spielberg's reputation as the greatest director of mass-appeal entertainment of his generation. And, unlike 99 percent of the directors on the planet, he became a household name. *E.T.* may well be his best-loved movie, and with good reason.

The film opens in a forest setting, where aliens are taking samples of Earth plants. When they hear men heading toward them, they hastily return to their spaceship and take off, leaving one creature behind. That night, the alien chances to meet Elliott, a wide-eyed ten-year-old boy played by Henry Thomas. Frightened at first, Elliott quickly realizes that the strange-looking visitor means him no harm and decides to hide—and protect—him. He shares this secret with his older brother and younger sister, but not his mom, whose nerves are frayed by the pain of going through a divorce.

In *E.T.*, Spielberg touched a nerve with every member of his audience, from the young to the young-at-heart. Who couldn't relate to this film and the family at its core? Many people who saw it when

Drew Barrymore's first reaction to seeing E.T. in the family closet

it debuted in the summer of 1982 now regard it with warm nostalgia and can't wait to share it with their children.

Henry Thomas is a charming Elliott whose work here seems completely natural—as was evident in his first screen test for Spielberg. Six-year-old Drew Barrymore is adorable as his kid sister, who shrieks when she first lays eyes on E.T. in her closet. Robert MacNaughton capably completes the complement of children. If we didn't like and respond to these ordinary suburban kids, the film would fall apart. Dee Wallace is especially good as the anxious mother—a recurring role in Spielberg's work, the reason for which becomes clear after watching his dramatized life story in *The Fabelmans* (2022). In the film, which he cowrote and directed, his parents' divorce is at the heart of the story (with Michelle Williams playing the highly emotional mother in an Oscar-nominated performance).

A directorial homage: When Elliott gets lightheaded in chemistry class, he grabs a fellow student (future starlet Erika Eleniak) and twirls her body around into an embrace—parroting a movie E.T. has just watched on television. This was Spielberg's tip of the hat to one of his heroes, John Ford, who directed the film that turns up in that television scene, *The Quiet Man* (1952), with John Wayne and Maureen O'Hara.

Nothing hurts films of the 1980s more than tacky music scores and even tackier visual effects. This picture avoids both of those pitfalls, as John Williams's orchestral score is one of his finest, and the effects team won a well-deserved Oscar for its work. Carlo Rambaldi (who designed the title creature), Dennis Muren, and Kenneth Smith shared the Academy Award for Best Visual Effects, while another two Oscars were presented to the sound team (Robert Knudson, Robert Glass, Dom Digirolamo, and Gene S. Cantamassa) and the two men responsible for sound effects editing, Charles S. Campbell and the legendary Ben Burtt.

No one anticipated the enormous worldwide success of this film. When Columbia Pictures did market research to see if people would be interested in a story about a boy and his alien friend, most of the respondents said no. How could they have envisioned what it turned out to be? Columbia terminated its option on the property, and it was made at Universal Pictures instead.

Among the other naysayers were the powers-that-be at M&Ms. The candymakers famously turned down the opportunity to have Elliott sprinkle their

Mom (Dee Wallace) comforts her son without truly understanding what's going on right under her nose.

Elliott and his neighborhood friends frantically try to protect E.T. from the "authorities," whoever they may turn out to be.

product on the ground in order to lure E.T. out of the toolshed in Elliott's backyard. The filmmakers used Reese's Pieces instead and boosted that brand's recognition enormously.

As a parent, Spielberg listened to complaints that the police and watchmen who figure in the climax of the story had guns in their hands and holsters. Why introduce the threat of gunplay or violence in such a tenderhearted film? When high-quality digital effects became available, the director manipulated every scene in question and substituted flashlights for guns.

There was a time when Hollywood wasn't afraid of sentimentality. Changes and upheavals in our society have made audiences more hard-boiled and cynical, but *E.T. the Extra-Terrestrial* invites us to shed tears. As the film reaches an emotional climax to the accompaniment of John Williams's brilliant music, even cynics have been known to succumb.

The film was honored with five Oscar nominations altogether, including Best

Picture, Best Director, Best Cinematography, and Best Original Screenplay. Screenwriter Melissa Mathison had already won praise for *The Black Stallion* (1979) and would go on to pen such worthy films as *Kundun* (1997), *The Indian in the Cupboard* (1995), and *The BFG*, which reunited her with Spielberg. Cinematographer Allen Daviau would earn four additional nominations for *The Color Purple* (1985), *Empire of the Sun* (1987), *Avalon* (1990), and *Bugsy* (1991), but never won. Producer Kathleen Kennedy has amassed eight Best Picture nominations, four with Spielberg, but has never won, although she was presented the prestigious Irving G. Thalberg Memorial Award in 2019.

As to Best Picture, the Academy was true to form and gave the majority of its prizes that year to an epic-scale historical drama, *Gandhi* (1982). This book's coauthor (Leonard) predicted on *Entertainment Tonight* that in the decades to come, *E.T.* would be cherished in a way that the perfectly respectable, well-made *Gandhi* would not. And I was right.

Steven Spielberg directing his young star, Henry Thomas

Chocolate Peanut Butter Pie

To honor E.T.'s love of Reese's Pieces, it's time to make a delicious peanut-buttery pie. You can buy a ready-made pie crust if you like or make one from scratch. For the crust, depending on your love of chocolate, you can use either regular graham crackers or chocolate ones. We love chocolate, so we're going with that.

MAKES 1 9-INCH PIE

FOR THE CRUST:

⅓ cup (⅔ stick) unsalted butter, melted

¼ cup brown sugar

¼ cup unsweetened cocoa powder

1¼ cups crushed-up chocolate graham crackers

FOR THE FILLING:

8 ounces cream cheese, at room temperature

1 cup confectioners' sugar, divided

1 cup creamy peanut butter

1 cup heavy whipping cream

1 teaspoon vanilla extract

1 bag chocolate peanut butter cups

Make your crust first. In a large bowl, combine the butter, brown sugar, cocoa powder, and crushed-up graham crackers. Press the mixture into a 9-inch pie tin. Chill the crust in the fridge while you prepare the filling.

Using an electric mixer, beat the cream cheese, ¾ cup of confectioners' sugar, and peanut butter until light and fluffy, about 3 minutes. Set the bowl aside.

In a separate bowl, using an electric mixer fitted with a whisk attachment, whip the cream until it thickens. Add in the remaining ¼ cup of confectioners' sugar and the vanilla extract and continue to whip for another couple of minutes, until stiff peaks form.

Gently fold the whipped cream into the peanut butter mixture. Pour into the prepared pie shell and freeze for 3 hours or chill in the fridge at least 6 hours.

Top with crumbled peanut butter cups and serve (no need to wait for it to come to room temperature).

Ralphie looks with pride at the fruit basket he's brought for his teacher.

A CHRISTMAS STORY

(1983)

93 MINUTES

Produced by René Dupont and Bob Clark | **Directed by** Bob Clark
Screenplay by Jean Shepherd and Leigh Brown | **Cinematography by** Reginald H. Morris
Music by Carl Zittrer and Paul Zaza | **Cast:** Melinda Dillon, Darren McGavin, Peter Billingsley, Ian Petrella, Scott Schwartz, Teddy Moore, Yono Anaya, Zack Ward; narrated by Jean Shepherd

Every now and then, a scene in a movie becomes iconic. Few kids (or adults) are likely to forget the moment when a boy gets his tongue stuck to an icy pole in the middle of winter. Even allowing for comic exaggeration, there's little in this movie that doesn't feel genuine. That's why word-of-mouth from the people who saw it in late 1983 prompted MGM to reissue it to theaters a year later, when it built an even bigger following. Repeated showings on cable TV then made it a genuine hit . . . and a bull's-eye for its creator, Jean Shepherd.

Shepherd carved a career for himself as a storyteller on radio, in print, in person, and in books that collected his essays. He never seemed to run out of material, recalling incidents from his youth and his idiosyncratic family. Thc TV scrics *The Wonder Years* baldly copied his style, with Daniel Stern taking his place as the narrator remembering his youth. But in this milestone movie, he came into his own.

Peter Billingsley plays Ralphie, the "hero" of the story, told as a series of flashbacks to the early 1940s. Darren McGavin is inspired as Ralphie's Old Man, who curses a blue streak but mumbles his words so no curses are ever actually audible. Melinda Dillon (still prominent to moviegoers of 1983 as one of the leads in 1977's *Close Encounters of the Third Kind*) is an ideal mom, long-suffering

Ralphie's visit to Santa at Higbee's department store doesn't end well.

to be sure. Ralphie has his heart set on getting a Red Ryder 200-shot BB gun for Christmas, but his mother repeatedly warns him that he's "going to shoot [his] eye out with that thing."

Everything about this movie rings true, even though it's a work of fiction. The period detail is impeccable, and it even stages a scene at Higbee's, long the leading department store in Cleveland, Ohio. When I (Leonard) was growing up in a Jewish family in New York, the only places that stayed open on Christmas Day were the Chinese restaurants, just like the film depicts.

Although much has changed about childhood since the 1940s, kids of today still relate to Ralphie, just as they do to the Little Rascals, because humor based on human faults and frailties is never out of date. It matters less that the leading character listens to radio shows than the fact that an advertiser makes him feel like he's been had. Who can't identify with that?

The saddest thing about *A Christmas Story* is that director Bob Clark and writer-narrator Jean Shepherd had a sequel ready to go called *My Summer Story*. The actors were eager to reprise their roles

It's true! If you try to lick a metal pole, your tongue will get stuck—maybe forever!

and everything was in place . . . but MGM would not make a commitment. Once Peter Billingsley grew older the opportunity was lost, and Darren McGavin was busy with other projects (he died in 2006). By the time the studio decided to make the second movie in 1994, the bloom was off the rose, and Charles Grodin was miscast as the Old Man. The film limped into theaters under two different titles, *My Summer Story* and *It Runs in the Family*. It's not a bad film by any means, but it can't touch the original.

Christmas Stir-Fry

As a Jewish family, we know that few things taste better than Chinese food on Christmas Day. We feel there's really no other way to celebrate! Let's get merry with this chicken stir-fry.

MAKES 4 SERVINGS

4 cups water

2 cups white rice

¾ cup soy sauce, divided

¼ cup brown sugar

1 tablespoon cornstarch

1 pound boneless skinless chicken breasts, cubed

1-inch piece fresh ginger, peeled and grated

1 head garlic, cloves separated and minced

Chili seasoning or sauce (optional)

2 tablespoons sesame oil, divided

1 cup sliced button mushrooms

1 small zucchini, sliced

1 cup broccoli, cut into florets

1 white onion, sliced

1 can water chestnuts, drained

1 large red bell pepper, chopped

1 can baby corn, drained

Sesame seeds, for garnish

Bring the water and rice to a boil in a medium saucepan. Reduce the heat to medium-low, cover, and simmer until rice is tender, around 20 minutes. Set aside.

In a large bowl, combine ½ cup of soy sauce, the brown sugar, and the cornstarch. Mix until smooth. Mix in the chicken, ginger, and garlic. (Add chili seasoning or sauce if you want a bit of spice.) Cover the bowl and chill in the refrigerator for 15 minutes.

Heat 1 tablespoon of sesame oil over medium-high heat in your wok (or skillet). Slowly add in all of your vegetables. Sauté, stirring frequently, until softened, about 5 to 7 minutes. Transfer the vegetables to a bowl.

To the same wok (or skillet), add the remaining sesame oil and your chicken mixture over medium-high heat and sauté, stirring frequently to ensure even browning. Add back in your vegetables and the remaining ¼ cup of soy sauce. Stir to combine.

Serve your stir-fry over rice and garnish with sesame seeds. It's good enough to eat any time of year.

Westley (Cary Elwes) and Buttercup (Robin Wright) are a perfect couple whose love for each other is undying.

THE PRINCESS BRIDE

(1987)

98 MINUTES

Directed by Rob Reiner | **Produced by** Norman Lear, Rob Reiner, Andrew Scheinman | **Screenplay by** William Goldman; based on his book **Cinematography by** Adrian Biddle | **Production design by** Norman Garwood **Music by** Mark Knopfler | **Cast:** Cary Elwes, Mandy Patinkin, Chris Sarandon, Christopher Guest, Wallace Shawn, Andre the Giant, Fred Savage, Robin Wright, Peter Falk, Peter Cook, Mel Smith, Carol Kane, Billy Crystal

"As you wish . . ."

How does one devise a brand-new fairy tale? That was the challenge that esteemed screenwriter William Goldman set for himself, with his two daughters in mind, when he wrote the novel *The Princess Bride.* A number of high-ranking producers and stars approached him about the movie rights, but he was in no hurry to make a deal. He wanted to find somebody who was simpatico and had the skills to translate his dreamlike story to film.

Rob Reiner and his writing and producing partner Andrew Scheinman persuaded him that they were the ones, and the result is there for all to see. If any component of the finished picture were removed or mishandled, *The Princess Bride* might not have the fervent following it enjoys today. It is still cherished and even quoted on a regular basis.

Instead of "Once upon a time . . ." this fairy tale unfolds as a flashback, with rumpled grandpa (a perfectly chosen Peter Falk) reading a book to his grandson (Fred Savage), who is home from school, sick in bed. The boy interrupts his grandpa's recitation from time to time, to object to kissing scenes and to clarify certain plot points that don't make sense to him.

Fred Savage as the grandson repeatedly interrupts his grandpa (Peter Falk), who is reading him *The Princess Bride*.

The tale is told of a beautiful young woman named Buttercup (Robin Wright) who falls in love with servant boy Westley (Cary Elwes) on the farm where she lives. She finally admits to her deep feelings for him, and he tells her that while he is going away to seek his fortune, he will always come back for her. After he leaves, word has it that he has lost his life on a pirate ship. Five years later, Buttercup is engaged to Prince Humperdinck (Chris Sarandon) and is abducted by a trio of petty criminals. A dashing Man in Black (Elwes) defeats one of the trio through swordplay (Mandy Patinkin), knocks out a colossus of a man (Andre the Giant), and bests the last (Wallace Shawn) in a battle of wits. This leaves our hero on his own just long enough to be captured by the Prince and his sneering henchman (Christopher Guest). The prince announces the impending nuptials, but Buttercup tells him he's wrong: she is going to be rescued by Westley. Can our hero beat the odds, regroup with his untrustworthy comrades, and penetrate the castle where Humperdinck and his guards stand ready? It will take a miracle to do so.

The Princess Bride isn't a "meta" film, but its self-awareness is part of its charm.

Yet for at least this viewer (Leonard), its parts are greater than the whole. There are sequences that dazzle the imagination: scaling the Cliffs of Insanity, walking through the Fire Swamp, battling the Rodents of Unusual Size, surviving the torture device known only as The Machine? Inconceivable!

By now, devotees know virtually all there is to know about the film: that Robin Wright (who is officially "introduced" in the cast list) was the last person to audition for her part, that Elwes and Patinkin worked tirelessly on their fencing scene and did not use stunt doubles, that director Reiner provided the scratchy voices of the ROUS, and that almost no one could keep from breaking up at the ad-libs spouted by Billy Crystal in his hilarious scene as Miracle Max. Mandy Patinkin

Cary Elwes channels Douglas Fairbanks as the Man in Black, who comes for Princess Buttercup, just as he promised.

Mandy Patinkin is the resourceful—and unstoppable—Inigo Montoya.

says that not a day goes by without someone approaching him and reciting his mantra, "Hello. My name is Inigo Montoya. You killed my father. Prepare to die!"

Many of the professionals who collaborated with Reiner on this film had truly impressive résumés, from two-time Oscar-winning costume designer Phyllis Dalton, who worked on *Lawrence of Arabia* (1962) and *Doctor Zhivago* (1965), to Bob Anderson, a fencing champion who coached everyone from Errol Flynn to Sean Connery—and stood in for Darth Vader in the original *Star Wars* movies.

Speaking of swashbucklers, when Westley becomes the Man in Black and sports a mustache, he closely resembles Hollywood's original swashbuckler, Douglas Fairbanks, as he looked in the 1920 silent-film classic, *The Mark of Zorro.* One of his costars, Christopher Guest, wasn't so much a lookalike as a soundalike for British character actor Henry Daniell, a memorably despicable villain in Errol Flynn's *The Sea Hawk* (1940).

Fans can't seem to get enough behind-the-scenes stories about this enduring endeavor. An official companion book was published in 2012, with a foreword by Rob Reiner and an afterword by executive producer Norman Lear. A more personal "making of" book written by star Cary Elwes (with Joe Leydon) called *As You Wish: Inconceivable Tales from the Making of The Princess Bride* was published in 2014, and yet another official tie-in book called *As You Wish: A Guided Journal Inspired by The Princess Bride* was published in 2021.

The film also inspired Billy Crystal to produce, cowrite, and star in a semi-autobiographical movie called *My Giant* (1998) about his relationship with Andre the Giant, the famous wrestler who plays Fezzik—and who died in 1993. It's not a great movie, but if you're a Crystal fan, it's worth seeing. Of *The Princess Bride* he has written, "I designed the makeup with Peter Montagna, who, at the time, had turned me into many different characters on *Saturday Night Live.* We decided the look was a combination of my grandma Sophie and [famous baseball manager] Casey Stengel."

Produced in the earliest days of CGI, before it was in regular use, this film relies instead on old-fashioned matte paintings—hand-painted on panes of glass—to establish and extend the scenery and sets where they shot the picture, in England and Ireland. The castle, however, is real.

All of the film's cast members feel grateful to have been a part of something as enduring as this. Producer and financier Norman Lear said it made him a hero to his children and grandchildren.

And Wallace Shawn, the cerebral playwright and lisping actor who plays Vizzini, wrote, "The gratitude people feel for entertainment is extraordinary and moving—a testament to human unhappiness, I suppose, and our powerful need for relief from it." Amen to that.

Toad-in-the-Hole

Rodents of Unusual Size love Yorkshire pudding, and we can't help but agree. It is magical and glorious, and we would eat it every day with everything. Some recipes call for British pork sausages, but we prefer mushrooms and beef. The key to making them is all temperature-based. It's a beautiful combination of meat and vegetables housed in the most delicious Yorkshire pudding.

MAKES 4 PUDDINGS

FOR THE YORKSHIRE PUDDING:

1½ cups whole milk

1¼ cups all-purpose flour

4 large eggs

½ teaspoon kosher salt

Beef tallow, beef fat, or goose fat

FOR THE FILLING:

1 tablespoon olive oil

3 tablespoons unsalted butter, divided

2 pounds beef chuck, chopped

8 ounces cremini mushrooms, sliced

1 large carrot, sliced

1 head garlic, cloves separated and minced

10 pearl onions

Kosher salt and freshly ground black pepper

4 tablespoons all-purpose flour

2 cups beef stock

Preheat the oven to 425°F. Add the milk, flour, eggs, and salt to a blender and mix. Set aside.

Place a muffin tin inside the oven. After about 5 minutes, remove the tin and coat the wells with beef tallow, beef fat, or goose fat. Return the tin to oven until the wells are piping hot and the fat is sizzling.

Remove the tin and pour in your pudding mixture, filling the wells about halfway. Bake the puddings for about 15 minutes, peering at them frequently to watch them rise. When they're golden brown, they're done.

Now it's time for your meat and gravy. Heat the oil and 1 tablespoon butter over medium-high heat in a large skillet. Add your beef and sauté for 4 to 5 minutes. Mix in half of your mushrooms, then slowly mix in the rest. Add your carrot, garlic, pearl onions, salt, and pepper. Stir to combine. Cook until everything in your pan is golden. (You may want to add in a little more butter as you adjust seasonings.) Transfer the contents of the skillet to a bowl and set aside.

Using the same skillet, add the remaining 2 tablespoons butter over medium heat. After the butter has melted, add in your flour, stirring frequently for 3 minutes. Pour in your beef stock and stir for 3 to 4 minutes, until the mixture comes together.

Add the beef and vegetables back in and adjust seasonings to taste. Pour over your Yorkshire puddings and serve.

Rick Moranis is in his element as Wayne Szalinski, a sort of absent-minded professor.

HONEY, I SHRUNK THE KIDS

(1989)

93 MINUTES

Directed by Joe Johnston | **Produced by** Penney Finkelman Cox
Screenplay by Ed Naha and Tom Schulman; from a story by Stuart Gordon, Ed Naha, Brian Yuzna | **Cinematography by** Hiro Narita | **Music by** James Horner
Cast: Rick Moranis, Marcia Strassman, Matt Frewer, Kristine Sutherland, Thomas Brown, Jared Rushton, Amy O'Neill, Robert Oliveri, Carl Steven, Mark L. Taylor, Frank Welker

There are so many unforgettable scenes in this movie, it's hard to pick a favorite: a boy swimming in a bowl of Cheerios, he and a friend riding an ant like a bucking bronco, a patch of grass that suddenly looks like an endless jungle. This is the epitome of movie magic: making the impossible come to life. Rick Moranis plays the "mad scientist" whose experimental machine shrinks his two sons and their neighbors into miniatures so tiny they can only be seen through a magnifying glass.

We don't want to give away any of this film's many surprises. But none of it would matter if we didn't believe in the main character, played with gusto by Rick Moranis. By this film's release, Moranis was a major comedy star and beloved by a young generation of fans who were familiar with his work in television (on Second City Television) and such films as *Ghostbusters* (1984) and *Little Shop of Horrors* (1986), and his pairing with Dave Thomas as the McKenzie Brothers in *Wayne's World* (1992). Here, he is called on to be a true absent-minded professor whose heart is always in the right place even if his technology is problematic. The one thing we never question is his sincerity.

Thomas Brown, Amy O'Neill, Robert Oliveri, and Jared Rushton are the shrunken kids.

The burden of carrying the story through a series of action sequences falls to the young actors playing the kids, and they are both likable and believable. Amy O'Neill and Robert Oliveri made their screen debuts as Moranis's children, while Jared Rushton (who costarred in *Big* with Tom Hanks in 1988) and Thomas Brown live next door. They have their spats and disagreements as any young foursome would, and Rushton begins to see his attractive neighbor in a different light than before.

But at its heart this is a survival story, played out on a grand scale. What's more, we feel what these accidental adventurers go through as if we're experiencing it ourselves. The film may have been made in the earliest stages of CGI, but by building oversized sets and using forced perspective, our attention is seldom, if ever, drawn away from the fundamental storyline. It all looks convincingly real.

Executive producer Thomas G. Smith, who supervised the effects in *E.T. the Extra-Terrestrial* and *Raiders of the Lost Ark*, said, "Nobody knew if we could pull it off, make people look small and make it look realistic. So we did tests of the kids riding an ant and another where they ran up a candy wrapper. They did the trick."

The entire film was shot in and around Churubusco Studios in Mexico City. Not one frame was exposed in the US. Churubusco is a huge facility that could easily encase two standard suburban houses side by side. Its capacity for a gigantic blue screen was also helpful in executing some effects scenes.

For film buffs, *Honey, I Shrunk the Kids* is also a valentine to old-school effects work, drawing on talents like Phil Tippett, who animated the scorpion one frame at a time (the same way his heroes brought *King Kong* to life in 1933), and matte painters like Mark Whitlock

These kids have no choice but to be brave.

Robert Oliveri in the most famous scene in *Honey, I Shrunk the Kids*

(son of legendary matte magician Albert Whitlock) and Syd Dutton and Bill Taylor of Illusion Arts.

It took a hardworking crew nine months to build all the props and sets you see. They didn't take shortcuts, and the results show how good they were. For the incredible Cheerios breakfast scene, they had to build a swimming-pool-sized cereal bowl and fill it with 16,000 gallons of make-believe milk, using chlorinated water, pigment, and a food product thickener. The O-shaped cereal bits were actually inner-tubes, painted and textured by production designer Gregg Fonseca, along with creatures and miniatures supervisor David Sosalla and mechanical effects coordinator Peter M. Chesney. And talk about old-school: some shots of the ant required the services of seven to twelve puppeteers!

The story was devised by Stuart Gordon (a major force in the Chicago theater scene, who is best remembered as the director of *The Re-Animator* in 1985), Brian Yuzna (who wrote and directed some *Re-Animator* sequels), and Ed Naha (who started as a journalist and founded *Fangoria* magazine). The finished film is credited to Naha and Tom Schulman, the Oscar-winning writer of *Dead Poets Society* (1985), *What About Bob?* (1991), and *Welcome to Mooseport* (2004), among others.

Rick Moranis couldn't have predicted that playing Wayne Szalinski would become a second career. *Honey, I Blew Up the Kid* followed in 1992, then *Honey, We Shrunk Ourselves* in 1997. That same year, Peter Scolari stepped into Wayne's shoes in a *Honey, I Shrunk the Kids* TV series that ran for three seasons. What's more, the movie was the inspiration for a wonderful attraction at Disneyland and other Disney theme parks called Honey, We Shrunk the Audience. It is one of the best 3D multimedia shows we have ever seen . . . and one that warranted repeat visits. Each time, we were greeted by Rick Moranis in an extension of his character and his penchant for things going wrong.

To direct this ambitious movie, Disney recruited Joe Johnston, who already had an impressive résumé at George Lucas's Industrial Light & Magic operation. Beginning as a concept artist on the first *Star Wars* trilogy, he helped to design the Millennium Falcon and the character of Boba Fett. He turned out to have a gift for communicating with actors as well as riding herd over a team of set and prop builders and real-life "mad scientists." He went on to direct a number of excellent films, including two of our family favorites, *October Sky* (1999) and *Hidalgo* (2004). He also piloted one of Marvel's best features, *Captain America: The First Avenger* (2011).

Interviewed at the time of the film's theatrical release, Johnston said, "Those of us who grew up in the fifties remember a special kind of Walt Disney film . . . wonderful excursions that spoke to the adventurous spirit, regardless of age. They were boldly stated films, not afraid to push the envelope of wonder and credibility, yet they had a certain kind of from-the-heart honesty. Through all the unusual perils of moviemaking, the challenge of *Honey, I Shrunk the Kids* was to capture that same kind of Disney electricity that makes an audience willingly lose itself in an impossible world."

Cheeri–OH NO! Bars

We find ourselves in a bit of a sticky sweet situation–this is our take on a Rice Krispies Treat. Adding in tiny people is usually optional, but we think that in this case it's necessary.

MAKES 12 BARS

¼ cup (½ stick) unsalted butter

3 cups mini marshmallows

2 cups Cheerios

Melt the butter in a large saucepan. Slowly add the mini marshmallows, stirring to keep from burning. If you want more of a caramel taste, keep on medium heat until the mixture starts to brown.

Remove from heat and slowly stir in the Cheerios until they are completely coated in your butter/marshmallow mixture.

Spoon mixture into a 9-inch square pan and lightly press it to fill the pan. Once cool, cut into bars.

We don't imagine one could buy wallet-sized copies of this family portrait at the mall.

THE ADDAMS FAMILY

(1991)

99 MINUTES

Directed by Barry Sonnenfeld | **Produced by** Scott Rudin
Screenplay by Caroline Thompson and Larry Wilson; based on characters created by Charles Addams | **Cinematography by** Owen Roizman
Music by Marc Shaiman | **Production design by** Richard Macdonald
Main titles designed by Pablo Ferro | **Cast:** Anjelica Huston, Raul Julia, Christopher Lloyd, Dan Hedaya, Elizabeth Wilson, Judith Malina, Carel Struycken, Dana Ivey, Paul Benedict, Christina Ricci, Jimmy Workman, Christopher Hart, John Franklin, Tony Azito

To watch Anjelica Huston and Raul Julia as Morticia and Gomez Addams is to witness perfect casting. Baby boomers who grew up on the 1960s TV series might argue for Carolyn Jones and John Astin, but Huston and Julia have more notes to play in this lavishly produced feature, a deep dive into the macabre world created by cartoonist Charles Addams.

This spooky-ooky comedy will serve as a litmus test for your family's sense of humor. It demonstrates that one shouldn't judge a book, or a family, by its appearance. They love each other and are kind and welcoming hosts but behave in a "kooky" manner that sets them apart.

Only parents can decide if their kids are ready for this brand of humor. If you're trying to explain the nature of the gags, think of what would be considered normal, and then anticipate these characters to do the exact opposite. One example: Morticia cuts a bowl of roses, trimming off the flowers and arranging the thorny stems in a vase.

Addams began using these characters in the spot cartoons he sold to *The New Yorker* magazine in the late 1930s. They developed a considerable following,

Gomez (Raul Julia) is thrilled to be reunited with his long-lost brother Uncle Fester (Christopher Lloyd).

and his drawings were soon collected in a series of hardcover books with titles like *Drawn and Quartered* and *Favorite Haunts*. His distinctive signature was reproduced by Pablo Ferro in the opening titles of this movie. It was the prospect of a TV series in 1964 that demanded they all acquire proper names: Morticia, Gomez, children Wednesday and Pugsley, Uncle Fester, butler Lurch, animated-hand Thing, and Grandma Addams. The series ran in prime time on ABC for two seasons, amassing sixty-four episodes. Its lasting contribution to popular culture is its theme song (complete with finger snaps, courtesy of composer Vic Mizzy).

This unique and bizarre household has had incredible "legs," leading to several television revivals (both live-action and animated) and a Broadway musical, where Nathan Lane played Gomez and Bebe Neuwirth was Morticia. In 2022, puppet master Tim Burton produced a streaming television series called *Wednesday*, focusing on the Addams's dark-humored daughter, played by Jenna Ortega. Catherine Zeta-Jones and Luis Guzmán fill in as her parents.

Still, no one could compare with Anjelica Huston and Raul Julia in this handsome feature. In a word I rarely use, they are perfect . . . and they knew it. Huston didn't blush as I (Leonard) paid her that compliment when the movie sequel was imminent; her smile was one of satisfaction rather than egocentricity. It's as if they were born to play these characters.

Dan Hedaya portrays their long suffering lawyer, Tully Alford, who is beholden to a greedy Abigail Craven (Elizabeth Wilson) and concocts a scheme to fleece the Addamses out of a fortune: having Abigail's adopted son Gordon (Christopher Lloyd) pretend to be Gomez's long-lost brother Fester. The return of his beloved sibling after so many years blinds Gomez into embracing his relative—while the rest of the family remains skeptical.

Morticia (Anjelica Huston) keeps the thorns but discards the roses in her solarium.

Pugsley (Jimmy Workman) and Wednesday (Christina Ricci) seem to be hatching a scheme with their Uncle Fester.

The Addams Family marked the directorial debut for cinematographer Barry Sonnenfeld, who had collaborated closely with the Coen brothers on their earliest films. He developed the shaky camera technique, put to excellent use here for point-of-view shots enabling us to scurry along the floors of the Addams house with the disembodied hand known as Thing.

The film, which was plagued with production problems, turned out to be a box-office and critical hit and yielded one of the few sequels in Hollywood history that is just as good as the original: *Addams Family Values*. Paul Rudnick, one of the greatest comedy writers of this generation, who had done rewrites on this script (credited to Caroline Thompson and Larry Wilson), received sole credit for *Addams Family Values*, which was released in 1993.

Thirty years after completing *The Addams Family*, director Sonnenfeld told Brent Lang of *Variety*, "One of the things I love about this movie is how romantic it is. It's also very pro-family. Every reviewer would write 'It's the most dysfunctional family.' Actually, no. It's a very functional family. The parents love their children. The children love their parents. The parents leave the children alone so they can grow and learn."

Black-as-My-Soul Pasta

In keeping with the Addams Family's dark view of life, we considered squid ink pasta, but let's be honest—we're scaredy cats. Instead, we present to you: black pasta. You have two options: you can buy pasta that is already black or dye it yourself. We went with the latter choice.

MAKES 4 SERVINGS

1 package pasta, any type

Blue, red, and green food dye

4 tablespoons (½ stick) salted butter

10 mushrooms, chopped

1 clove garlic, minced

1 (12-ounce) package zucchini noodles or 2 medium zucchini, spiralized

Onion powder

Kosher salt and freshly ground black pepper

Poppy seeds

Cook the pasta according to package instructions. Transfer the drained pasta to an airtight plastic container and add a bit of blue, red, and green food dye. Shake to combine, then set aside.

In a large skillet, melt the butter over medium. Add the mushrooms, garlic, and zucchini noodles, sautéing until browned. Add the black pasta, onion powder, salt, and pepper and stir to combine, then remove from heat.

Sprinkle black poppy seeds on top and serve. It's a dish Morticia would dye for.

Mary's first encounter with Colin is anything but cordial—or promising.

THE SECRET GARDEN

(1993)

101 MINUTES

Directed by Agnieszka Holland | **Produced by** Fred Fuchs, Tom Luddy, Fred Roos
Screenplay by Caroline Thompson; based on the novel by Frances Hodgson Burnett
Cinematography by Roger Deakins | **Production design by** Stuart Craig
Music by Zbigniew Preisner | **Cast:** Kate Maberly, Hayden Prowse, Andrew Knott, Maggie Smith, Laura Crossley, John Lynch, Walter Sparrow, Irene Jacob

Any child who saw this movie at an impressionable age has dreamed of having their own secret garden. Seeing it through young Kate Maberly's eyes brings it to life in a truly memorable way. It's just one example of how the novels written by Frances Hodgson Burnett still yield rich rewards in their adaptations to film, from the silent era to the present day: *A Little Princess* (1995), *Little Lord Fauntleroy* (1936), and *The Secret Garden.*

The sumptuous 1993 production was directed by Agnieszka Holland, a versatile Polish filmmaker who was chosen by executive producer Francis Ford Coppola with an eye toward bringing a European sensibility to this material. It was also imperative that she have a gift for working with child actors.

The time is 1901, and the story is told by ten-year-old Mary Lennox (Kate Maberly), who lives with her parents in India. Her mother and father have little to do with her, and she feels unloved. One night, as she hides under her mother's bed, an earthquake strikes, and she is suddenly orphaned. Mary is sent to live in a mansion in Yorkshire, England, owned by her uncle Lord Archibald Craven (John Lynch) . . . but she is warned by prickly housekeeper Mrs. Medlock (Maggie Smith) that it is highly unlikely she will ever meet her uncle,

The formidable, even fearsome, Mrs. Medlock, played by Maggie Smith

who travels most of the time. The house is eerie and filled with strange sounds, such as a little boy crying. When curiosity overtakes Mary, Mrs. Medlock sends her outside, where she discovers her late aunt's walled garden, which has been locked for a decade. She makes friends with Dickon (Andrew Knott), whose sister is one of the manor's housemaids, and the more time they spend together inside the garden, the happier they become. In time they learn that the crying they hear is coming from a boy named Colin (Heydon Prouse), Mary's ill-tempered cousin, who has been confined to a bed and a wheelchair all his life by his father—though no one knows what's wrong with him. Mary and Dickon bring him inside the garden, and in due course, the three become close friends, although they hide this from the grown-ups—especially Colin's father. As the garden blooms, so do the three children.

This is a lovely film that captures all the offbeat qualities of Burnett's novel and, through thoughtful casting and beautiful location work in Yorkshire, gives us the feeling of having an experience as opposed to merely watching a movie. This was the result of a serendipitous blend of talents. *The Secret Garden* was an American Zoetrope presentation, which means it was executive produced by Francis Ford Coppola. One of the producers, Fred Fuchs, recalls that they

This is the isolated world that Colin inhabits until Mary comes into his life.

struggled with Warner Bros. to keep the setting from being moved to America and to prevent "name" actors like Thora Birch and Elijah Wood from being cast. They felt the Britishness of the book had to be maintained at all costs.

They chose Agnieszka Holland after seeing her films *Europa/Europa* (1990) and especially *Olivier/Olivier* (1992), where she worked so well with children. The screenplay was written by an American, Caroline Thompson. Her impressive credits include *Edward Scissorhands* (1990), *The Addams Family*, *The Nightmare Before Christmas* (1993), and another literary adaptation, *Black Beauty* (1994).

The mostly unknown cast was selected with care. The one readily recognizable person on-screen is Maggie Smith, who is (it must be said) typecast as the waspish Mrs. Medlock. If Dame Maggie hadn't existed, someone would have had to invent her to play her signature roles, including Mrs. Medlock and Professor McGonagall in the *Harry Potter* series.

The film was beautifully shot by English-born cinematographer Roger Deakins, a two-time Oscar winner who is best known for his long association with the Coen brothers on such memorable films as *Fargo* (1996), *The Big Lebowski* (1998), and *No Country for Old Men* (2007). He refuses to be typecast, however,

Over the course of time, the garden has a different meaning to each of the children who adopt it as their own. Kate Maberly, Andrew Knott, and Hayden Prowse bring Frances Hodgson Burnett's distinctive characters to life.

and has shot films as diverse as *Kundun* (1997) and *1917* (2019). His extraordinary skill is put to the test in this period piece, set at the dawn of the twentieth century in an ominous mansion, where the darkened corridors are contrasted with the beauty of a grand English garden that comes to life right before our eyes.

The principal characters are extremely well drawn, although they represent a handful of recognizable social archetypes. You might ask your family if they have ever encountered a spoiled snob like Mary (as she is when she first arrives at the castle) or a hypochondriac like Colin, who has convinced himself that he can't walk and shouldn't breathe fresh air. We hope you haven't suffered an acquaintance with anyone like the formidable Mrs. Medlock. I (Leonard) had one of them as a teacher in the sixth grade.

The Secret Garden has been filmed many times, inspiring sequels and at least two television series in England, in 1960 and 2010. The best known is the 1949 MGM production starring Margaret O'Brien, Dean Stockwell, and Herbert Marshall. It's not bad, but it takes liberties with the novel and is not as nuanced as this remake. In an era of black-and-white filmmaking, its most notable quality was showcasing the garden scenes in Technicolor.

Tea Party in the Garden

There's never a bad time for a tea party, and it's the perfect way to get creative. Dickon, Mary, and Colin would surely love to spend some time picking fresh ingredients with you in the garden. Enjoy the results at your leisure; don't ever rush a tea party.

MAKES 4 SERVINGS

Loose leaf or bagged tea of choice

Loaf of artisan bread (anything that makes you feel fancy)

TOPPINGS OF CHOICE:

Tomatoes, cucumber, red onion, figs, apples, avocado, lox, canned tuna, etc.

SPREADS OF CHOICE:

Cheeses, jams, nut butters, butter, etc.

SEASONINGS OF CHOICE:

Chives, dill, salt, pepper, etc.

This "recipe" is actually all up to you and your imagination. All you need to do is pick out your ingredients, prep everything the way you like, and enjoy. Feel free to toast your bread or leave as is. Maybe try softened cheese topped with slices of fig or cream cheese with cucumbers, cherry tomatoes, and fresh dill on top. If you have any little ones, you can make Jessie's personal favorite—fairy bread! Made popular in Australia, you take a piece of white bread, spread it with butter, and then cover it with rainbow sprinkles. What could be bad about that?

Grab yourself a cup of tea and indulge in all of these happy treats.

Mary has vivid memories of her privileged life in India.

A LITTLE PRINCESS

(1995)

97 MINUTES

Directed by Alfonso Cuarón | **Produced by** Mark Johnson
Cinematography by Emmanuel Lubezki | **Production design by** Bo Welch
Music by Patrick Doyle | **Cast:** Liesel Matthews, Eleanor Bron, Liam Cunningham, Rusty Schwimmer, Arthur Malet, Vanessa Lee Chester, Errol Sitahal, Heather DeLoach, Camilla Belle, Vincent Schiavelli

A 1905 novel by the perennially popular Frances Hodgson Burnett inspired this lavish production, which helped to launch the career of Mexican director Alfonso Cuarón, who went on to make *Children of Men* (2006), *Gravity* (2013), and *Harry Potter and the Prisoner of Azkaban* (2004). Even people who haven't read the book may be familiar with the story, which was tailored for Shirley Temple in 1939 and filmed in Technicolor. Because its copyright wasn't renewed, that version has fallen into the public domain and is ubiquitous on home video, cable, and streaming channels. But while it covers the same basic ground as the book, it is engineered as a star vehicle for Temple, while the 1995 remake is a lavish, lovingly detailed production and a more faithful rendering of Burnett's original story.

In 1914, a widowed British Army officer takes his young daughter from India—which makes a deep and lasting impression on her—to New York and places her in a fancy orphanage while he goes off to fight in the Great War. The elegant old mansion is run by a cruel headmistress named Mrs. Minchin (Eleanor Bron). Sara is given the premium suite, and her gift for telling fantastic stories makes her popular with the other girls, including a Black servant named Becky. One day, a lawyer shows up bearing the terrible news that Sara's father has been killed

Life at the orphanage seems happy—at first.

in battle. Knowing that this means she will not be receiving any more monthly checks, the headmistress tells Sara that in order to stay she must work as a servant. She moves the girl to a seedy attic room and filches her most prized possession, a locket with a picture of her mother inside. Perched up high near the roof of the orphanage, Sara becomes acquainted with the Indian servant who takes care of the elderly owner of the townhouse next door. The owner is badly shaken when a wounded soldier is misidentified as his son, but his servant persuades him to allow the fallen soldier to recuperate in the comfort of his mansion. Suffering from amnesia, the soldier is unaware of how close he is to his own daughter.

Any superior movie relies on good casting, and this film has no weak links. Eleanor Bron, who is so well remembered by baby boomers for her costarring role in The Beatles' *Help!* (1965), is an ideal Mrs. Minchin, consistently menacing but never a caricature of a villain. But it is the luminous and completely natural performance of Liesel Matthews as Sara that draws us in and makes us care. The other girls follow her lead and don't overplay their parts or attempt to compete with the film's protagonist, just as the other grown-ups (mostly incidental in nature) capably fill their roles.

This film marked a turning point for filmmaker Alfonso Cuarón, who made such an impression on producer Mark

The forbidding headmistress of the orphanage, played by Eleanor Bron

Johnson with his work in Mexico and his first Hollywood gig (a TV movie produced by Sydney Pollack), that he persuaded Warner Bros. to hire a relative newcomer to direct this multimillion-dollar production. Johnson made sure that Cuarón was surrounded by skilled specialists, and two of them—costume designer Judianna Makovsky and cinematographer Emmanuel Lubezki—received Academy Award nominations for their work. The final screenplay was credited to Richard LaGravenese and Elizabeth Chandler.

Echoing the Shirley Temple movie, the skies are not always blue in this rendition of the novel. War is real and not an abstract, and though the battlefront scenes are brief, they still have a dramatic impact. The same is true for visions of India, mystical dreams, and flashbacks that are incredibly vivid.

Casting is always a challenge for any filmmaker, but especially with stories in which the protagonist is a child. Liesel Matthews chose not to parlay her completely natural performance here into a full-time career, and we are the poorer for it. She is warm and winning from the first scene to the last.

In real life, Matthews inherited the Pritzker family fortune and has become a noted philanthropist. She certainly didn't amass that money from the receipts of this film, which, despite excellent reviews, fared poorly at the box office. Yet it stands as one of the finest literary adaptations in modern memory.

Becky (Vanessa Lee Chester) finds common ground with newcomer Sara (Liesel Matthews) at the boardinghouse that becomes their prison.

Chicken Tikka Masala

Sara's love of India and its beautiful spices inspired us to try making one of Britain's most beloved dishes—chicken tikka masala. An important tip we've learned: the longer you let the chicken soak in the marinade, the better it will taste.

MAKES 4 SERVINGS

FOR THE MARINADE:

1½ pounds boneless skinless chicken breasts, cubed

½ cup whole Greek yogurt

1 teaspoon kosher salt

¼ teaspoon freshly ground black pepper

½ tablespoon garam masala

FOR THE CHICKEN TIKKA MASALA:

4 tablespoons (½ stick) butter, divided

1 yellow onion, diced

1 tablespoon garam masala

1 tablespoon paprika

½ teaspoon turmeric

½ teaspoon cayenne pepper

2 garlic cloves, minced

1-inch piece fresh ginger, peeled and minced

1 (14.5-ounce) can crushed tomatoes

½ cup coconut milk

Naan bread and basmati rice, for serving

Parsley and/or cilantro, for garnish

Make the marinade: In a large bowl, combine the chicken, yogurt, salt, pepper, and garam masala. This marinade can sit for as little as 20 minutes or be refrigerated in an airtight container overnight.

In a large pot, melt 2 tablespoons of butter over medium heat. Add the chicken and sauté, browning evenly. Transfer to a plate and set aside.

Melt 2 more tablespoons of butter in the pot, then add the onion. Sauté until translucent. Stir in the garam masala, paprika, turmeric, cayenne, garlic, and ginger.

Add the crushed tomatoes and chicken and stir to combine. Cover the pot and let it simmer for roughly 15 minutes.

Stir in the coconut milk and adjust seasonings to taste.

Serve with naan and basmati rice. Garnish with parsley and/or cilantro.

It all begins here, with Daniel Radcliffe as the boy wizard Harry Potter.

HARRY POTTER AND THE SORCERER'S STONE

(2001)

152 MINUTES

Directed by Chris Columbus | **Produced by** David Heyman
Screenplay by Steve Kloves; based on the novel by J. K. Rowling
Cinematography by John Seale | **Production design by** Stuart Craig
Music by John Williams | **Cast:** Daniel Radcliffe, Rupert Grint, Emma Watson, Richard Harris, Maggie Smith, Robbie Coltrane, Fiona Shaw, Richard Griffiths, John Cleese, Ian Hart, Alan Rickman, Warwick Davis, Verne Troyer, John Hurt, Julie Walters, Tom Felton, Zoë Wanamaker, voice of Leslie Phillips

Harry Potter changed the world. Suddenly, a vast number of young people were excited about reading books in a whole new way. It was a phenomenon never seen before: kids (and their parents) were lining up at bookstores for the midnight release of each book in J. K. Rowling's series. They raced through them in record time before friends could spoil any of the surprises waiting for them. Adults soon followed, as *Harry Potter* became watercooler conversation and no one wanted to be left out. The books left TV shows and movies in the dust.

If anything marks the passage of time, it's the fact that the *Harry Potter* series is now decades old, and its incomparable cast of children are now adults. Many of the costars who filled colorful roles right out of the pages of Rowling's books have passed away. But the movies remain, eight amazing chapters in a saga like no other in entertainment history. Tarzan and James Bond have had longer lives on-screen, but no one has ever produced a series based on best-selling books that

The three musketeers of Hogwarts: Harry, Ron Weasley, and Hermione Granger

follow the same characters, played by the same actors, over the span of a decade. It has no precedent.

The first adaptation reached the screen four years after the novel was released in 1997. Each installment in the series was hefty and filled with characters and incidents. Die-hard fans complained about what was missing, but there was simply too much in each book to fit into a feature film. In a twenty-first century media landscape, *Harry Potter* would get the miniseries treatment, which could pack more into eight or ten episodes than one could expect in a theatrical feature.

But the complaints were drowned out by the acclaim that greeted the movies, especially when it came to casting. Beginning in 2001 and continuing through the end of the decade, we all watched Daniel Radcliffe, Rupert Grint, and Emma Watson grow up right before our eyes.

What's more, they matured as actors, working alongside many of the finest performers in Great Britain. It got to a point where if you had achieved any success or status in the UK and weren't asked to participate, you would have every right to consider yourself insulted.

Every story has a beginning, and it would make no sense to start anywhere but there. *Harry Potter and the Sorcerer's Stone* (titled *Harry Potter and the Philosopher's Stone* in the UK and elsewhere) introduces us to young Harry and his cruel aunt and uncle, the Dursleys. We witness the moment he learns that he is a wizard, and a gifted one at that. It isn't surprising that he is happy to leave his family behind and board the train at Station 9¾ for Hogwarts School of Witchcraft and Wizardry—after stocking up on school supplies, like a wand.

While riding on the train to Hogwarts, Harry meets the two people who are destined to be his closest friends, Ron Weasley and Hermione Granger. When they arrive and are sorted into their dormitories, all three are housed in Gryffindor.

From that point forward, the film offers an endless array of surprising sights and

Competition is fierce at Hogwarts.

Harry and his newest friend

sounds, from a three-headed dog to the first of many quidditch matches. (How much fun would it be to join in?) There is the Cloak of Invisibility, the enchanted chessboard, and so much more.

The supporting cast is unbeatable. Richard Harris is Professor Dumbledore; Maggie Smith is Minerva McGonagall, his deputy headmistress; Robbie Coltrane is Hagrid, the gamekeeper and groundskeeper; Alan Rickman is Severus Snape, who seems to have it in for Harry; Fiona Shaw and Richard Griffiths are Harry's aunt and uncle; John Hurt is Ollivander, who makes and sells magic wands; John Cleese is Nearly Headless Nick, a ghost; Julie Walters is Ron Weasley's mother; and Warwick Davis is Filius Flitwick (as well as the goblin head teller at Gringotts and the voice of Griphook). Tom Felton sneers his way through the series as Draco Malfoy, Zoë Wanamaker is the school's flying instructor, and veteran actor Leslie Phillips provides the voice of the Sorting Hat.

They would be joined by new characters and top-ranked British actors to play them in each subsequent chapter of the Harry Potter saga.

Do the films live up to the books that

spawned them? Nothing can compare to the joy of reading, the intensely personal experience of taking in the author's words and imagining the faces and images being described. But as much as any movie can, we believe this series captures the essence of J. K. Rowling's work on the printed page.

Producer David Heyman had his choice of almost any director alive. He chose Chris Columbus, whose résumé included the screenplays for *Gremlins* (1984), *The Goonies* (1985), and *Home Alone* (1990) and the directorial duties for *Home Alone* and *Mrs. Doubtfire* (1993). He set the stage for everything that followed; it was also Columbus who saw Daniel Radcliffe and insisted that he was the right person to play Harry Potter.

Steve Kloves, who wrote and directed *Racing with the Moon* (1984) and *The Fabulous Baker Boys* (1989), and also wrote *Wonder Boys* (2000), provided the screenplays for all but one of the eight *Harry Potter* films, which must set some sort of record for productivity, not to mention excellence.

If you and your family have not been exposed to Harry Potter, you have a treat and a privilege awaiting you. You can decide whether you want to read (or listen to) the books first or simply enjoy the movies. There is no entrance exam to do so. But know this: in any medium, this outpouring of imagination will leave a lasting impression on the young and young-at-heart in your family.

Potter's Pumpkin Pasties

Pasties can be savory or sweet, shoved into robe pockets or served on a platter. You can even give your pasties a Harry Potter–style scar. The possibilities are endless. We've provided instructions for four servings; if you can do the math, you can make as many as you like. Be sure to buy pie crust dough that's not pre-formed.

MAKES 4 PASTIES

Store-bought pie crust dough, at room temperature

FOR THE FILLING:

1 cup unsweetened pumpkin purée

1 large egg

2 tablespoons honey

1 teaspoon vanilla extract

⅛ teaspoon cloves

⅛ teaspoon nutmeg

¼ teaspoon cinnamon

⅛ teaspoon kosher salt

¼ cup brown sugar

2 tablespoons mascarpone cheese

FOR THE GLAZE (OPTIONAL):

1 teaspoon vanilla extract

3 tablespoons of milk

1 cup confectioners' sugar

Preheat the oven to 400°F. Line a baking sheet with parchment paper.

Roll out the pie crust dough and cut into four equal circles. Set aside.

Pour the pumpkin purée onto a paper towel to soak up some of the moisture (this is a pro tip for pumpkin pie, too). Add the pumpkin purée to a large bowl along with the rest of your filling ingredients. Gently stir to combine.

Using a small spoon, fill one half of each pasty with the pumpkin mixture. Keep the filling to one side and do not overfill.

Pasties are also known as hand pies because you can form them with your hands. Wet the tips of your fingers, then gently lift the edges on the unfilled side of the pasty and fold it over the other half, creating a semicircle. Crimp the edges with your fingertips or a fork to make sure your filling is sealed inside.

If you want your pasties to be extra sweet, make the glaze. In a small bowl, combine the vanilla, milk, and confectioners' sugar. Brush it on top of your pastry before putting in the oven.

Bake for 22 minutes, or until golden brown. Let cool before serving.

Seeing is believing: this fairy-tale princess is the real thing.

ENCHANTED

(2007)

107 MINUTES

Directed by Kevin Lima | **Produced by** Barry Sonnenfeld and Barry Josephson
Screenplay by Bill Kelly | **Songs by** Alan Menken and Stephen Schwartz
Score by Alan Menken | **Cinematography by** Don Burgess
Production design by Stuart Wurtzel | **Costume design by** Mona May
Animated scenes directed by James Baxter | **Cast:** Amy Adams, Patrick Dempsey, James Marsden, Susan Sarandon, Timothy Spall, Idina Menzel, Rachel Covey, Julie Andrews

If you're going to introduce your family to a new, real-life princess, she had better be as lovable and convincing as Amy Adams is in *Enchanted*. That's just one reason this movie is so special. For our family, any film that promotes kindness is cause for celebration. It doesn't try to reinvent the wheel; it embraces the classic Walt Disney fairy tales, while going them one better as its animated characters come to life. The musical numbers are joyful and worth watching more than once. They make you smile, and that's a rare quality in movies nowadays. Princess Giselle's greatest gift is teaching the people around her to appreciate every moment. She makes everyone she meets feel special.

This aptly titled Disney movie is a disarming mix of fairy tale and real life. In fact, it's about a collision between the two. Amy Adams is a versatile actress who has played scientists and stressed-out mothers, but she has cornered the market on pure-hearted heroines like Giselle. She's the princess who leads this story, from her home of Andalasia to the streets of New York City. What's more, while she's an animated character for the first eleven minutes of the picture, she emerges from a Times Square manhole in human form, wearing her tiara and poofy wedding dress.

Prince Edward proposes to Giselle as her new friends look on in disbelief.

Not many actresses could pull this off without winking at the audience, but Adams remains wide-eyed and innocent about the ways of the world. What's more, we believe her. The same can't be said for a single dad (Patrick Dempsey) who doesn't believe she's for real . . . any more than he would think to read a fairytale book to his cute daughter Morgan (Covey). Giselle's Prince (James Marsden) follows her path to Times Square, as does the villainous Queen Narissa's bumbling henchman (Timothy Spall). They are all greeted with cynicism and disbelief, and when the henchman's attempts to do away with the princess fail, the Queen (Susan Sarandon) reluctantly makes the journey herself to guarantee her dominance over a waffling Magic Mirror.

Enchanted is about a clash between a world of make-believe and what we all recognize as modern life. Which side does your family lean toward? Age and degree of adult responsibility will have a lot to do with everyone's choices.

Patrick Dempsey, then at the height of his popularity as "McDreamy" on television's *Grey's Anatomy*, is well cast as the unbeliever who nevertheless takes the lost princess into his home at the urging of his daughter. He thaws further as the story moves along toward a spectacular (if not entirely necessary) action finale atop a Manhattan skyscraper.

The film is buoyed by a sparkling song score written by Disney legend Alan Menken (*The Little Mermaid*, *Beauty and the Beast*) and Stephen Schwartz (*Pocahontas*, *The Hunchback of Notre Dame*, and *Wicked*). Two of its three standout songs were nominated for Oscars, but not the one that might have taken home the gold: "True Love's Kiss."

"That's How You Know" is set in Central Park and begins as Giselle trades lines with a three-man reggae band. Soon every performer and park visitor joins in to make this a spectacular musical event. The good vibes that the princess projects are apparently infectious. Bravo to choreographer John O'Connell, who staged this rousing number with scores of smiling participants.

Bill Kelly's script is filled with visual and verbal gags, some of them aimed at kids and some that will likely fly over

Susan Sarandon, as the evil Queen, lays down the law for the romantic Prince Edward (James Marsden).

their heads and elicit a smile or chuckle from grown-ups in the room.

But it's the attention to detail that really enhances this valentine to Walt Disney and his renditions of classic fairy tales. From the traditional oversized storybook that opens to reveal intricate pop-up tableaux to the reassuringly familiar-sounding narrator, Julie Andrews, *Enchanted* is meant to revive the spirit of those indelible films, while gently kidding some of their conventions, such as forest animals gathering to help Snow White—except here they are unappealing city residents from the animal and insect kingdom. As an inside joke for Disneyphiles, it's fun to try spotting the women who provided singing voices for Ariel (Jodi Benson), Pocahontas (Judy Kuhn), and Belle (Paige O'Hara), though only Benson has a full scene with dialogue as Dempsey's receptionist.

Director Kevin Lima had a long history with Disney when he accepted this assignment. He started out as an animator and character designer on such features as *The Great Mouse Detective* (1986) and *Oliver & Company* (1988) and rose through the ranks to direct *A Goofy Movie* (1995), *Tarzan* (1999, with Chris Buck), and his live-action debut, *102 Dalmatians* (2002). If anyone was sufficiently well-versed in Disney tradition and lore, it was he. (In the film, a neon sign for a restaurant advertises Bella Notte, the name of the establishment where the two leading characters eat spaghetti and meatballs in 1955's *Lady and the Tramp*.)

Animation producer James Baxter had worked at the studio but eventually hung out his own shingle. Timing was on his side, because some of Disney's leading artists like Andreas Deja and Mark Henn were between assignments and available to freelance. That's how Baxter and his team achieved the look of bona fide Disney animation. Then it was up to costume designer Mona May to fabricate costumes for Amy Adams and James Marsden that looked exactly like the ones in the cartoon footage—but wearable for the duration of filming. They cost a small fortune to produce. The single most expensive garment was the all-leather, skin-hugging gown worn by Susan Sarandon for the climax of the movie. It ran up a bill of $75,000.

Enchanted is a wonderful postscript to classic Disney animated films, but when the stars reunited to make *Disenchanted* in 2022, lightning did not strike again. To adopt Giselle's positive point of view, that simply makes the original 2007 movie that much more precious.

Tempting (and Harmless) "Poison" Candy Apples

Giselle couldn't resist, and neither will you. It's just an apple, after all . . . And if you're really tempted, you can adjust the recipe to make as many candy apples as your heart desires.

MAKES 4 SERVINGS

4 wooden skewers

4 apples (Honeycrisp or Granny Smith)

2 cups granulated sugar

1 cup cold water

¼ cup corn syrup

Beet juice or red food dye

⅛ teaspoon cinnamon

⅛ teaspoon vanilla extract

Candy thermometer (optional)

Line a baking sheet with parchment paper. Insert the skewers into your apples.

In a medium saucepan over high heat, combine the remaining ingredients and stir, bringing to a boil. Once boiling, stop stirring. You need your sugar mixture to get to 300°F so that it will form a hard coating on your apple. Use a meat or candy thermometer to track the temperature. It should take about 10 to 15 minutes.

Once at temperature, remove from heat. After the bubbles have dissipated, you're ready to start dipping. Coat your apples evenly and then place them on the baking sheet.

Once the apples have cooled completely, they're ready to enjoy.

ACKNOWLEDGMENTS

The authors would like to thank:

From TCM: Lindsey Griffin, Genevieve McGillicuddy, Aaron Spiegeland, Matthew Ownby, Katie Daniels, and John Malahy.

From Running Press: Our editor, Cindy Sipala, as well as Amanda Richmond, Seta Zink, Betsy Hulsebosch, Amy Cianfrone, Shannon Fabricant, Leah Gordon, and Doug Wolff.

Our families and friends, especially Steven Smith, Craig Barron, Howard Green, James Curtis, Kevin Kern, Jeremy Arnold, Jeremy Patrich, and Alonso Duralde.

INDEX

Note: Page reference in italics indicate photographs.

A

The Addams Family (1991)
- cast/scenes, *150*, 151–154, *152*, *153*, *154*
- director/producer, 151, 154
- plot/background, 151–154
- recipe: Black-as-My-Soul Pasta, 155, *155*

apples
- Tea Party in the Garden, 161, *161*
- Tempting (and Harmless) "Poison" Candy Apples, 183, *183*

B

bacon
- Calam's Biscuits, *66*, 67
- "Good Morning" Breakfast for Dinner, *58*, 59
- Harper Lee's Crackling Cornbread, *80*, 81

beef
- beef broth, 15, 51, 75, 141
- Brooklyn Corned Beef and Cabbage, 51, *51*
- German Goulash for the Monster in All of Us, *14*, 15
- Lightsaber Skewers, *118*, 119
- Milly's Stick-to-Your-Ribs Stew, *74*, 75
- Toad-in-the-Hole, *140*, 141

bell peppers
- Christmas Stir-Fry, *132*, 133
- Doggone-Good Gumbo, 111, *111*
- German Goulash for the Monster in All of Us, *14*, 15
- Lightsaber Skewers, *118*, 119
- "Somewhere Over the Rainbow" Pizza, *30*, 31

Biscuits, Calam's, *66*, 67

Black-as-My-Soul Pasta, 155, *155*

bread
- Calam's Biscuits, *66*, 67
- "Good Morning" Breakfast for Dinner, *58*, 59
- Harper Lee's Crackling Cornbread, *80*, 81
- Tea Party in the Garden, 161, *161*

breakfast
- Calam's Biscuits, *66*, 67
- Cheeri–OH NO! Bars, *148*, 149
- Coogan Cakes, 7, *7*
- "Good Morning" Breakfast for Dinner, *58*, 59

Bride of Frankenstein (1935)
- cast/scenes, *8*, 9–13, *10*, *11*, *12*
- director/producer, 9–11
- plot/background, 9–13
- recipe: German Goulash for the Monster in All of Us, *14*, 15

broccoli
- Christmas Stir-Fry, *132*, 133
- "Somewhere Over the Rainbow" Pizza, *30*, 31

Brooklyn Corned Beef and Cabbage, 51, *51*

broth
- beef broth, 15, 51, 75, 141

Brooklyn Corned Beef and Cabbage, 51, *51*
chicken broth, 97, 111
Doggone-Good Gumbo, 111, *111*
German Goulash for the Monster in All of Us, *14*, 15
Milly's Stick-to-Your-Ribs Stew, *74*, 75
One of Maria's Favorite Things . . ., *96*, 97
Toad-in-the-Hole, *140*, 141

C

Cabbage and Corned Beef, 51, *51*
cakes/cupcakes
Hickory Nut Cake, *44*, 45
National Velvet Carrot Cake Cupcakes, 38–39, *39*
Pineapple Upside-Down Cake, *88*, 89
Splendiferously Indulgent Cupcakes, *104*, 105
Calamity Jane (1953)
cast/scenes, *60*, 61–65, *62*, *63*
director/producer, 61, 64
plot/background, 61–65
recipe: Calam's Biscuits, *66*, 67
Calam's Biscuits, *66*, 67
Candy Apples, Tempting (and Harmless) "Poison," 183, *183*
Captain January (1936)
cast/scenes, *16*, 17–21, *18*, *21*
director/producer, 17–18
plot/background, 17–21
recipe: Captain's Fish Sandwich, *22*, 23
Captain's Fish Sandwich, *22*, 23
Carrot Cake Cupcakes, 38–39, *39*
carrots
Brooklyn Corned Beef and Cabbage, 51, *51*
German Goulash for the Monster in All of Us, *14*, 15
Milly's Stick-to-Your-Ribs Stew, *74*, 75
National Velvet Carrot Cake Cupcakes, 38–39, *39*
Toad-in-the-Hole, *140*, 141
celery
Doggone-Good Gumbo, 111, *111*
Milly's Stick-to-Your-Ribs Stew, *74*, 75
Cheeri–OH NO! Bars, *148*, 149
cheese
Calam's Biscuits, *66*, 67
Potter's Pumpkin Pasties, *176*, 177
"Somewhere Over the Rainbow" Pizza, *30*, 31
Tea Party in the Garden, 161, *161*
chicken
chicken broth, 97, 111
Chicken Schnitzel, *96*, 97
Chicken Tikka Masala, *168*, 169
Christmas Stir-Fry, *132*, 133
Doggone-Good Gumbo, 111, *111*
Lightsaber Skewers, *118*, 119
One of Maria's Favorite Things . . ., *96*, 97
chili sauce
Christmas Stir-Fry, *132*, 133
Chocolate Peanut Butter Pie, *126*, 127
Christmas Stir-Fry, *132*, 133
A Christmas Story (1983)
cast/scenes, *128*, 129–131, *130*, *131*
director/producer, 129–130
plot/background, 129–131
recipe: Christmas Stir-Fry, *132*, 133
cinnamon
Coogan Cakes, 7, *7*
Hickory Nut Cake, *44*, 45
National Velvet Carrot Cake Cupcakes, 38–39, *39*
Potter's Pumpkin Pasties, *176*, 177
Tempting (and Harmless) "Poison" Candy Apples, 183, *183*

Coogan Cakes, 7, *7*
Cornbread, Harper Lee's Crackling, *80*, 81
Corned Beef and Cabbage, 51, *51*
Cupcakes, *National Velvet* Carrot Cake, 38–39, *39*
Cupcakes, Splendiferously Indulgent, *104*, 105

D

desserts/treats
- Cheeri–OH NO! Bars, *148*, 149
- Chocolate Peanut Butter Pie, *126*, 127
- Hickory Nut Cake, *44*, 45
- *National Velvet* Carrot Cake Cupcakes, 38–39, *39*
- Pineapple Upside-Down Cake, *88*, 89
- Potter's Pumpkin Pasties, *176*, 177
- Splendiferously Indulgent Cupcakes, *104*, 105
- Tempting (and Harmless) "Poison" Candy Apples, 183, *183*

Doggone-Good Gumbo, 111, *111*

E

eggplant
- "Somewhere Over the Rainbow" Pizza, *30*, 31

eggs
- "Good Morning" Breakfast for Dinner, *58*, 59

Enchanted (2007)
- cast/scenes, *178*, 179–182, *180*, *181*
- director/producer, 179, 182
- plot/background, 179–182
- recipe: Tempting (and Harmless) "Poison" Candy Apples, 183, *183*

E.T. the Extra-Terrestrial (1982)
- cast/scenes, *120*, 121–125, *122*, *123*, *124*, *125*
- director/producer, 121–125, *125*
- plot/background, 121–125
- recipe: Chocolate Peanut Butter Pie, *126*, 127

F

fish
- Captain's Fish Sandwich, *22*, 23
- Doggone-Good Gumbo, 111, *111*
- Tea Party in the Garden, 161, *161*

fruit
- Pineapple Upside-Down Cake, *88*, 89
- Tea Party in the Garden, 161, *161*
- Tempting (and Harmless) "Poison" Candy Apples, 183, *183*
- *see also specific fruit*

G

Garden Tea Party, 161, *161*

garlic
- Black-as-My-Soul Pasta, 155, *155*
- Brooklyn Corned Beef and Cabbage, 51, *51*
- Calam's Biscuits, *66*, 67
- Captain's Fish Sandwich, *22*, 23
- Chicken Tikka Masala, *168*, 169
- Christmas Stir-Fry, *132*, 133
- Doggone-Good Gumbo, 111, *111*
- German Goulash for the Monster in All of Us, *14*, 15
- Lightsaber Skewers, *118*, 119
- Milly's Stick-to-Your-Ribs Stew, *74*, 75
- One of Marla's Favorite Things . . ., *96*, 97
- Toad-in-the Hole, *140*, 141

ginger
- Chicken Tikka Masala, *168*, 169
- Christmas Stir-Fry, *132*, 133
- *National Velvet* Carrot Cake Cupcakes, 38–39, *39*

"Good Morning" Breakfast for Dinner, *58*, 59

Goulash for the Monster in All of Us, *14*, 15
graham crackers
  Chocolate Peanut Butter Pie, *126*, 127
Gumbo, Doggone-Good, 111, *111*

H

Harper Lee's Crackling Cornbread, *80*, 81
Harry Potter and the Sorcerer's Stone (2001)
  cast/scenes, *170*, 171–175, *172*, *173*, *174*
  director/producer, 171, 175
  plot/background, 171–175
  recipe: Potter's Pumpkin Pasties, *176*, 177
Hickory Nut Cake, *44*, 45
Honey, I Shrunk the Kids (1989)
  cast/scenes, *142*, 143–147, *144*, *145*, *146*
  director/producer, 143, 147
  plot/background, 143–147
  recipe: Cheeri–OH NO! Bars, *148*, 149

J

jalapeño peppers
  Doggone-Good Gumbo, 111, *111*

K

The Kid (1921)
  cast/scenes, 1–6, *2*, *3*, *4*, *5*
  director/producer, 1–6
  plot/background, 1–6
  recipe: Coogan Cakes, 7, *7*

L

Lightsaber Skewers, *118*, 119
A Little Princess (1995)
  cast/scenes, *162*, 163–167, *164*, *165*, *167*
  director/producer, 163, 165–166
  plot/background, 163–167
  recipe: Chicken Tikka Masala, *168*, 169

M

main dishes
  Black-as-My-Soul Pasta, 155, *155*
  Brooklyn Corned Beef and Cabbage, 51, *51*
  Captain's Fish Sandwich, *22*, 23
  Chicken Schnitzel, *96*, 97
  Chicken Tikka Masala, *168*, 169
  Christmas Stir-Fry, *132*, 133
  Doggone-Good Gumbo, 111, *111*
  German Goulash for the Monster in All of Us, *14*, 15
  "Good Morning" Breakfast for Dinner, *58*, 59
  Lightsaber Skewers, *118*, 119
  Milly's Stick-to-Your-Ribs Stew, *74*, 75
  One of Maria's Favorite Things . . ., *96*, 97
  "Somewhere Over the Rainbow" Pizza, *30*, 31
  Tea Party in the Garden, 161, *161*
  Toad-in-the-Hole, *140*, 141
Mary Poppins (1964)
  cast/scenes, *82*, 83–87, *84*, *85*, *86*
  director/producer, 83
  plot/background, 83–87
  recipe: Pineapple Upside-Down Cake, *88*, 89
Masala, Chicken Tikka, *168*, 169
Meet Me in St. Louis (1944)
  cast/scenes, *40*, 41–43, *42*, *43*
  director/producer, 41–43
  plot/background, 41–43
  recipe: Hickory Nut Cake, *44*, 45
Milly's Stick-to-Your-Ribs Stew, *74*, 75
mushrooms
  Black-as-My-Soul Pasta, 155, *155*
  Christmas Stir-Fry, *132*, 133
  Lightsaber Skewers, *118*, 119
  Toad-in-the-Hole, *140*, 141

N

National Velvet (1944)
- cast/scenes, *32*, 33–37, *34*, *36*
- director/producer, 33, 35
- plot/background, 33–37
- recipe: Carrot Cake Cupcakes, 38–39, *39*

National Velvet Carrot Cake Cupcakes, 38–39, *39*

noodles
- Black-as-My-Soul Pasta, 155, *155*
- One of Maria's Favorite Things . . ., *96*, 97

nuts
- Hickory Nut Cake, *44*, 45
- *National Velvet* Carrot Cake Cupcakes, 38–39, *39*

O

One of Maria's Favorite Things . . ., *96*, 97

onions
- Brooklyn Corned Beef and Cabbage, 51, *51*
- Chicken Tikka Masala, *168*, 169
- Christmas Stir-Fry, *132*, 133
- Doggone-Good Gumbo, 111, *111*
- German Goulash for the Monster in All of Us, *14*, 15
- Lightsaber Skewers, *118*, 119
- Milly's Stick-to-Your-Ribs Stew, *74*, 75
- "Somewhere Over the Rainbow" Pizza, *30*, 31
- Tea Party in the Garden, 161, *161*
- Toad-in-the-Hole, *140*, 141

P

pancakes
- Coogan Cakes, 7, *7*

pasta
- Black-as-My-Soul Pasta, 155, *155*

Pasties, Potter's Pumpkin, *176*, 177

Peanut Butter Chocolate Pie, *126*, 127

peppers
- bell peppers, 15, 31, 111, 119, 133
- cayenne pepper, 169
- Chicken Tikka Masala, *168*, 169
- Christmas Stir-Fry, *132*, 133
- Doggone-Good Gumbo, 111, *111*
- German Goulash for the Monster in All of Us, *14*, 15
- jalapeño peppers, 111
- Lightsaber Skewers, *118*, 119
- "Somewhere Over the Rainbow" Pizza, *30*, 31

pies/pasties
- Chocolate Peanut Butter Pie, *126*, 127
- Potter's Pumpkin Pasties, *176*, 177

Pineapple Upside-Down Cake, *88*, 89

pizza
- "Somewhere Over the Rainbow" Pizza, *30*, 31

pork
- Calam's Biscuits, *66*, 67
- Doggone-Good Gumbo, 111, *111*
- "Good Morning" Breakfast for Dinner, *58*, 59
- Harper Lee's Crackling Cornbread, *80*, 81
- Toad-in-the-Hole, *140*, 141

potatoes
- Brooklyn Corned Beef and Cabbage, 51, *51*
- Lightsaber Skewers, *118*, 119
- Milly's Stick-to-Your-Ribs Stew, *74*, 75

Potter's Pumpkin Pasties, *176*, 177

The Princess Bride (1987)
- cast/scenes, *134*, 135–139, *136*, *137*, *138*
- director/producer, 135, 137–139
- plot/background, 135–139
- recipe: Toad-in-the-Hole, *140*, 141

Pumpkin Pasties, Potter's, *176*, 177

R

red wine
German Goulash for the Monster in All of Us, *14*, 15
Milly's Stick-to-Your-Ribs Stew, *74*, 75
rice
Chicken Tikka Masala, *168*, 169
Christmas Stir-Fry, *132*, 133
Doggone-Good Gumbo, 111, *111*
roux
Doggone-Good Gumbo, 111, *111*

S

sandwiches
Captain's Fish Sandwich, *22*, 23
sauces
Captain's Fish Sandwich, *22*, 23
chili sauce, 133
Christmas Stir-Fry, *132*, 133
Doggone-Good Gumbo, 111, *111*
pizza sauce, 31
roux, 111
"Somewhere Over the Rainbow" Pizza, *30*, 31
soy sauce, 133
tartar sauce, 23
sausage
Doggone-Good Gumbo, 111, *111*
Toad-in-the-Hole, *140*, 141
seafood
Captain's Fish Sandwich, *22*, 23
Doggone-Good Gumbo, 111, *111*
Tea Party in the Garden, 161, *161*
The Secret Garden (1993)
cast/scenes, *156*, 157–160, *158*, *159*, *160*
director/producer, 157–159
plot/background, 157–160
recipe: Tea Party in the Garden, 161, *161*
Seven Brides for Seven Brothers (1954)
cast/scenes, *68*, 69–73, *70*, *71*, *73*
director/producer, 69–71
plot/background, 69–73
recipe: Milly's Stick-to-Your-Ribs Stew, *74*, 75
shrimp
Doggone-Good Gumbo, 111, *111*
Singin' in the Rain (1952)
cast/scenes, *52*, 53–57, *54*, *55*, *56*, *57*
director/producer, 53–57, *57*
plot/background, 53–57
recipe: "Good Morning" Breakfast for Dinner, *58*, 59
Skewers, Lightsaber, *118*, 119
"Somewhere over the Rainbow" Pizza, *30*, 31
The Sound of Music (1965)
cast/scenes, *90*, 91–95, *92*, *93*, *94*
director/producer, 91–94
plot/background, 91–95
recipe: One of Maria's Favorite Things . . ., *96*, 97
Sounder (1972)
cast/scenes, *106*, 107–110, *108*, *109*, *110*
director/producer, 107, 110
plot/background, 107–110
recipe: Doggone-Good Gumbo, 111, *111*
Splendiferously Indulgent Cupcakes, *104*, 105
Star Wars (1977)
cast/scenes, *112*, 113–117, *114*, *115*, *116*
director/producer, 113–117
plot/background, 113–117
recipe: Lightsaber Skewers, *118*, 119
stews/soups
Doggone-Good Gumbo, 111, *111*
German Goulash for the Monster in All of Us, *14*, 15
Milly's Stick-to-Your-Ribs Stew, *74*, 75

Stir-Fry, Christmas, *132*, 133
syrups
Calam's Biscuits, *66*, 67
corn syrup, 183
maple syrup, 67
Tempting (and Harmless) "Poison" Candy Apples, 183, *183*

T

tartar sauce
Captain's Fish Sandwich, *22*, 23
Tea Party in the Garden, 161, *161*
Tempting (and Harmless) "Poison" Candy Apples, 183, *183*
Tikka Masala, Chicken, *168*, 169
To Kill a Mockingbird (1962)
cast/scenes, *76*, 77–79, *78*, *79*
director/producer, 77, 78
plot/background, 77–79
recipe: Harper Lee's Crackling Cornbread, 81, *80*
Toad-in-the-Hole, *140*, 141
tomatoes
Chicken Tikka Masala, *168*, 169
"Somewhere Over the Rainbow" Pizza, *30*, 31
Tea Party in the Garden, 161, *161*
A Tree Grows in Brooklyn (1945)
cast/scenes, *46*, 47–50, *48*, *49*, *50*
director/producer, 47–48
plot/background, 47–50
recipe: Brooklyn Corned Beef and Cabbage, 51, *51*

V

vegetables
Black-as-My-Soul Pasta, 155, *155*
Cabbage and Corned Beef, 51, *51*
Christmas Stir-Fry, *132*, 133
Doggone-Good Gumbo, 111, *111*
German Goulash for the Monster in All of Us, *14*, 15
Lightsaber Skewers, *118*, 119
Milly's Stick-to-Your-Ribs Stew, *74*, 75
"Somewhere over the Rainbow" Pizza, *30*, 31
Tea Party in the Garden, 161, *161*
Toad-in-the-Hole, *140*, 141
see also specific vegetable
vegetarian dishes
Black-as-My-Soul Pasta, 155, *155*
"Somewhere Over the Rainbow" Pizza, *30*, 31
Tea Party in the Garden, 161, *161*
vinegar
balsamic vinegar, 67
Calam's Biscuits, *66*, 67
Captain's Fish Sandwich, *22*, 23
German Goulash for the Monster in All of Us, *14*, 15
red wine vinegar, 15
white wine vinegar, 23

W

white wine
One of Maria's Favorite Things . . ., *96*, 97
Willy Wonka and the Chocolate Factory (1971)
cast/scenes, *98*, 99–103, *100*, *102*
director/producer, 99, 101–103
plot/background, 99–103
recipe: Splendiferously Indulgent Cupcakes, *104*, 105
wine
German Goulash for the Monster in All of Us, *14*, 15
Milly's Stick-to-Your-Ribs Stew, *74*, 75
One of Maria's Favorite Things . . ., *96*, 97

red wine, 15, 75
white wine, 97
The Wizard of Oz (1939)
cast/scenes, *24*, 25–29, *26*, *27*, *28*, *29*
director/producer, 25
plot/background, 25–29
recipe: "Somewhere Over the Rainbow" Pizza, *30*, 31

Y

Yorkshire Pudding, *140*, 141

Z

zucchini
Black-as-My-Soul Pasta, 155, *155*
Christmas Stir-Fry, *132*, 133